Test Bank

A Pocket Guide to Public Speaking

Dan O'Hair
Hannah Rubenstein
Rob Stewart

Prepared by

Elaine Wittenberg
University of Oklahoma

and

Merry Buchanan
Texas Christian University

BEDFORD / ST. MARTIN'S

Boston ♦ New York

Copyright © 2004 by Bedford/St. Martin's

All rights reserved.

Instructors who have adopted *A Pocket Guide to Public Speaking* as a textbook for a course are authorized to duplicate portions of this manual for their students.

Manufactured in the United States of America.

8 7 6 5 4
f e d c b a

For information, write: Bedford/St. Martin's, 75 Arlington Street, Boston, MA 02116   (617-399-4000)

ISBN: 0-312-41689-X

PREFACE

The *Test Bank* to accompany *A Pocket Guide to Public Speaking* contains over 1500 true/false, multiple-choice, fill-in-the-blank, and essay/short answer questions. The questions have been carefully crafted to test students' specific knowledge of the text. Also available is an Electronic Test Bank containing all of the test questions in a format that allows instructors to add their own questions and generate their own tests. The electronic version is available in Windows and Macintosh platforms. For more information on this ancillary, please call or write Bedford/St. Martin's, Faculty Services, 4B Cedarbrook Drive, Cranbury, NJ 08512 (866-843-3715), or contact your local Bedford/St. Martin's sales representative through our Web site, www.bedfordstmartins.com.

CONTENTS

Test Bank

A Pocket Guide to Public Speaking

Becoming a Public Speaker *1*

TRUE/FALSE QUESTIONS

1. Learning to speak effectively can enhance your career as a student.

2. Communication skills top the list of job skills sought by most employers.

3. Unlike many forms of communication, public speaking usually occurs in formal settings.

4. The source, or sender, is the person who receives the message.

5. Organizing the message, choosing words and sentence structures, and verbalizing the message is termed *encoding*.

6. The receiver decodes or interprets the message.

7. The content of a message can be expressed both verbally and nonverbally.

8. Another term for noise is *interference*.

9. Noise is the medium through which a speaker sends a message.

10. The channel is the content of the communication process.

11. Shared meaning is the mutual understanding of a message between speaker and audience.

12. A speech does not need a clearly defined goal to be effective.

13. The belief that the ways of one's own culture are superior to those of other cultures is called *ethnocentrism*.

14. The practice of oratory, or rhetoric, emerged full force in Greece in the fifth century B.C.E.

15. According to Aristotle and Cicero, memory is one of the five parts of speech preparation.

16. *Delivery* refers to adapting speech information to the audience in order to make your case.

17. The five canons of rhetoric are invention, adaptation, arrangement, timing, and delivery.

MULTIPLE-CHOICE QUESTIONS

18. Benefits of public speaking do *not* include
    A) exploring and sharing values.
    B) honing thinking and listening skills.
    C) improving hand-eye coordination.
    D) accomplishing professional and personal goals.

19. A form of communication between two people is called
    A) mass communication.
    B) small group communication.
    C) dyadic communication.
    D) public speaking.

20. In this form of communication, the receiver is physically removed from the messenger, and feedback is delayed.
    A) mass communication
    B) small group communication
    C) public speaking
    D) dyadic communication

21. Which of the following is the least formal type of communication?
    A) mass communication
    B) small group communication
    C) dyadic communication
    D) public speaking

22. All communication events include
    A) a source and a message.
    B) only a message.
    C) a transmittal device.
    D) none of the above.

23. Which of the following represents the process a message goes through when it is received and interpreted?
    A) channel → receiver → decoding
    B) source → receiver → encoding → decoding
    C) source → encoding → receiver → decoding
    D) source → receiver → channel

24. Transforming ideas and thoughts into messages is called
    A) encoding.
    B) decoding.
    C) receiving.
    D) channeling.

25. The recipient of the source's message is
    A) the encoder.
    B) the channel.
    C) the receiver.
    D) all of the above.

26. The audience's response to a message is referred to as
    A) shared meaning.
    B) feedback.
    C) the medium.
    D) decoding.

27. When setting goals for a speech, the speaker should ask himself
    A) What do I want the audience to learn or believe?
    B) What do I personally want to achieve by delivering this speech?
    C) both A and B.
    D) neither A nor B.

28. The belief that the ways of one's own culture are superior to those of other cultures is called
    A) ethnicity.   C) ethnocentrism.
    B) ethnography.   D) egocentrism.

29. Which of the following is *not* one of the five canons of rhetoric?
    A) invention   C) persuasion
    B) delivery   D) arrangement

30. *Invention* refers to
    A) adapting speech information to the audience in order to make your case.
    B) the way the speaker uses language to express the speech's ideas.
    C) practicing the speech until it can be artfully delivered.
    D) none of the above.

FILL-IN-THE-BLANK QUESTIONS

31. In a recent survey of employers, _____ communication skills ranked first among desired skills.

32. A form of communication between two people, such as a conversation, is _____ communication.

33. _____ is the process of interpreting a message.

34. The mutual understanding of a message between the speaker and the audience is called _____ .

35. _____ is the audience's verbal or nonverbal responses to a message.

36. _____ , also called noise, is a barrier to communication that may be physical, emotional, psychological, or environmental.

37. The opposite of ethnocentrism is _____ .

ESSAY AND SHORT ANSWER QUESTIONS

38. Explain how studying the craft of public speaking will hone your critical thinking and listening skills.

39. Discuss the shared characteristics of mass communication and public speaking.

40. List and describe one similarity and one difference between public speaking and small group communication.

41. Explain why public speaking is usually more formal than other types of communication.

42. Give an example of interference in a public speaking situation.

43. Why is it important for speakers to clearly define their goals?

44. List and describe three of the five canons of rhetoric.

ANSWER KEY FOR CHAPTER 1

1. True (p. 2)	16. False (p. 5)	31. oral (p. 2)
2. True (p. 2)	17. False (p. 5)	32. dyadic (p. 2)
3. True (p. 3)	18. C (p. 2)	33. Decoding (p. 3)
4. False (p. 3)	19. C (p. 2)	34. shared meaning (p. 4)
5. True (p. 3)	20. A (p. 2)	35. Feedback (p. 3)
6. True (p. 3)	21. C (p. 2)	36. Interference (p. 4)
7. True (p. 3)	22. A (p. 3)	37. cultural sensitivity (p. 7)
8. True (p. 4)	23. C (p. 4)	38. (No answer, p. 2)
9. False (p. 4)	24. A (p. 3)	39. (No answer, p. 2)
10. False (p. 4)	25. C (p. 3)	40. (No answer, p. 2)
11. True (p. 4)	26. B (p. 3)	41. (No answer, p. 3)
12. False (p. 5)	27. C (p. 5)	42. (No answer, p. 4)
13. True (p. 7)	28. C (p. 7)	43. (No answer, p. 5)
14. True (p. 5)	29. C (p. 5)	44. (No answer, p. 5)
15. True (p. 5)	30. A (p. 5)	

2 Ethical Public Speaking

TRUE/FALSE QUESTIONS

1. Public speakers are in a position to influence others but are not responsible for the effects their words have on listeners.

2. The Greek word *ethos* means character.

3. The First Amendment of the U.S. Constitution guarantees freedom of speech.

4. Listeners tend to distrust speakers who do not appear credible.

5. If a particular type of speech is legal, it is also ethical.

6. For the most part, values are culturally determined and transmitted through social institutions and organizations.

7. Most values are learned late in life and tend to remain with individuals for a short period of time.

8. Successful speeches appeal to the listeners' values.

9. The qualities of dignity and integrity are central to ethical speech.

10. Trustworthiness is a combination of honesty and dependability.

11. A respectful speaker focuses on issues as well as on personalities.

12. Manipulating information to achieve a particular purpose is not always unethical.

13. Acknowledging sources is an essential aspect of ethical speechmaking.

14. Racist, sexist, and ageist slurs are forms of hate speech.

15. Hate speech is directed solely against people's racial characteristics.

16. The quality of fairness in a speaker refers to his or her efforts to see all sides of an issue and be open-minded.

17. Any source that requires credit in written form should be acknowledged in oral form.

18. Verbatim statements are known as paraphrases.

19. It is not necessary to acknowledge direct quotations in a speech.

20. Paraphrasing alters the form but not the substance of another person's ideas.

21. Plagiarism is the act of crediting sources in a speech.

MULTIPLE-CHOICE QUESTIONS

22. Which of the following is a Greek word meaning character?
    A) logos
    B) ethos
    C) pathos
    D) mythos

23. Which of the following types of speech are legally protected in the United States?
    A) racist and sexist speech
    B) pornographic speech
    C) both A and B
    D) neither A nor B

24. The _____ Amendment assures protection to both honest and dishonest speakers.
    A) First
    B) Third
    C) Second
    D) Fourth

25. An ethical speaker is conscious of _____ values.
    A) the speaker's
    B) the speaker's and the university's
    C) the speaker's and the audience's
    D) the speaker's and all other people's

26. A person's feeling of worth, honor, or respect is called
    A) trustworthiness.
    B) dignity.
    C) integrity.
    D) candor.

27. An incorruptible speaker, or one who will not compromise solely to persuade others, possesses
    A) trustworthiness.
    B) dignity.
    C) integrity.
    D) candor.

28. A speaker who is both honest and dependable has the quality of
    A) trustworthiness.
    B) dignity.
    C) integrity.
    D) candor.

29. A speaker who is trustworthy
    A) does not use misleading information.
    B) reveals his or her true purpose.
    C) both A and B.
    D) neither A nor B.

30. Hate speech is offensive communication that is most often directed against
    A) political ideas.
    B) people's values.
    C) people's racial, ethnic, religious, gender, or other characteristics.
    D) people's psychological characteristics.

31. If a source used in a speech requires credit in written form, it also
    A) requires consent from the author.
    B) should be mentioned before the speaker's findings.
    C) needs to be quoted directly.
    D) should be acknowledged orally as another person's work.

32. To conduct a plagiarism check for your speech, you should do all of the following *except*
    A) acknowledge other people's research and evidence.
    B) acknowledge your own ideas and opinions.
    C) acknowledge direct quotations.
    D) acknowledge paraphrased information.

FILL-IN-THE-BLANK QUESTIONS

33. _____ are people's most enduring judgments about what is good or bad, important or unimportant.

34. A person's feeling of worth, honor, or respect is called _____ .

35. _____ is a quality that combines honesty and dependability.

36. _____ is offensive communication directed against people's race, ethnic origin, religion, gender, or other characteristics.

37. If a person uses someone else's ideas or words without acknowledging the source, he or she is committing _____ .

38. To _____ is to restate someone else's ideas, opinions, or theories in the speaker's own words.

ESSAY AND SHORT ANSWER QUESTIONS

39. Identify three personal values you feel you have in common with your classmates.

40. How can a speaker display the qualities of dignity and integrity during a speech?

41. Define *plagiarism* and provide an example.

42. List two elements of information a speaker should provide when citing sources during a speech.

43. Paraphrase this quotation: "The tongue weighs practically nothing, therefore people can hold it."

ANSWER KEY FOR CHAPTER 2

1. False (p. 7)	16. True (p. 9)	31. D (p. 10)
2. True (p. 8)	17. True (p. 10)	32. B (p. 10)
3. True (p. 8)	18. False (p. 11)	33. Values (pp. 8–9)
4. True (p. 8)	19. False (p. 11)	34. dignity (p. 9)
5. False (p. 8)	20. True (p. 11)	35. Trustworthiness (p. 9)
6. True (pp. 8–9)	21. False (p. 10)	36. Hate speech (pp. 9–10)
7. False (pp. 8–9)	22. B (p. 8)	37. plagiarism (p. 10)
8. True (pp. 8–9)	23. C (p. 8)	38. paraphrase (p. 11)
9. True (p. 9)	24. A (p. 8)	39. (No answer, pp. 8–9)
10. True (p. 9)	25. C (pp. 8–9)	40. (No answer, p. 9)
11. False (p. 9)	26. B (p. 9)	41. (No answer, p. 10)
12. False (p. 9)	27. C (p. 9)	42. (No answer, p. 10)
13. True (p. 10)	28. A (p. 9)	43. (No answer, p. 11)
14. True (pp. 9–10)	29. C (p. 9)	
15. False (pp. 9–10)	30. C (pp. 9–10)	

Listeners and Speakers *3*

TRUE/FALSE QUESTIONS

1. In any given communication situation, all listeners will process information in exactly the same way.

2. Selective perception is a process in which listeners pay attention to certain messages and ignore others.

3. Audience members usually listen carefully to a speaker even if they believe the message is of no consequence to them.

4. Active listening is focused and purposeful.

5. A listening distraction is anything that competes for attention you are trying to give to something else.

6. Noise, movement, light, darkness, heat, and cold are all examples of internal distractions.

7. When you experience strong emotions as you listen, these can be considered distractions.

8. Scriptwriting usually occurs when we sense that our attitudes or opinions are being challenged.

9. In defensive listening, audience members decide to hear things that aren't actually said by the speaker.

10. Laziness and overconfidence are concepts related to defensive listening.

11. Differences in dialects or accents, nonverbal cues, and physical appearance sometimes serve as cultural barriers to listening.

12. Active listeners listen for the speaker's main ideas and watch his or her nonverbal cues.

13. Setting listening goals helps listeners get the most from a listening situation.

14. Identifying a speaker's organizational pattern will help listeners understand the main points of a message.

15. When evaluating evidence, the listener should determine if the sources of the evidence are credible.

16. When listening to a speech, it is important to consider different perspectives and realize that both the listener's and the speaker's perspectives are subject to error.

17. Listeners who do not like a speaker's topic are not required to be honest and fair in evaluating the speech.

MULTIPLE-CHOICE QUESTIONS

18. Listeners tend to pay attention to
    A) information that they deem important.
    B) information that is associated with their experiences.
    C) information that relates to their backgrounds.
    D) all of the above.

19. Paying attention to information that is important to us, being interested in information that touches our own experiences and backgrounds, and sorting and filtering new information based on what we already know are key elements of
    A) imaginative listening.   C) simplistic listening.
    B) selective listening.   D) attentive listening.

20. Active listening is
    A) a vague, abstract multistep process.
    B) a focused, purposeful multistep process.
    C) a time-consuming one-step process.
    D) an active and engaging one-step system.

21. Distractions to listening can originate
    A) only outside of us.   C) both A and B.
    B) within our thoughts and feelings. D) neither A nor B.

22. Construction noise, automobile traffic, slamming doors, and poor ventilation are examples of
    A) external distractions.   C) defensive listening.
    B) internal distractions.   D) inattentiveness.

23. Daydreaming, fatigue, illness, and strong emotions are examples of
    A) scriptwriting.   C) external distractions.
    B) internal distractions.   D) defensive listening.

24. Scriptwriters tend to
    A) focus on the speaker.
    B) concentrate on the speaker's motives.
    C) plan how they will respond to the speaker.
    D) employ external distractions.

25. Laziness and overconfidence in listening are manifested by
    A) expecting too little from the speaker.
    B) displaying an arrogant attitude.
    C) ignoring important information.
    D) all of the above.

26. Active listeners
    A) are often distracting to other listeners.
    B) normally set listening goals and listen for main ideas.
    C) rely primarily on a speaker's verbal cues.
    D) apply the same goals to every speech.

27. When listening for main ideas, a listener should
    A) ignore the speaker's organizational pattern.
    B) take into account only the introduction, transitions, and conclusion.
    C) take notes of the speaker's main points.
    D) do none of the above.

FILL-IN-THE-BLANK QUESTIONS

28. Paying attention to certain messages and ignoring others is called _____ .

29. Anything that competes for the attention you are trying to give to something else is called a listening _____ .

30. Setting listening _____ helps active listeners get the most from the speaker's message.

ESSAY AND SHORT ANSWER QUESTIONS

31. Describe the factors that influence listening.

32. Explain why people sort and filter information based on what they already know.

33. Describe how a listener can plan ways of coping with common listening distractions.

34. Describe two types of internal distractions, and explain how they detract from a communication situation.

35. How does scriptwriting differ from defensive listening?

36. From your own experience, identify something you perceive to be a cultural barrier to listening.

37. Write a brief list of ways you can become a more active listener. Tailor these goals to your own strengths and weaknesses as a listener.

38. Identify three guidelines for evaluating speeches and presentations.

39. When you evaluate a speech, how can you be compassionate in your criticism?

ANSWER KEY FOR CHAPTER 3

1. False (p. 13)	14. True (p. 15)	27. C (p. 15)
2. True (p. 13)	15. True (p. 16)	28. selective perception (p. 13)
3. False (p. 13)	16. True (p. 16)	29. distraction (pp. 13–14)
4. True (p. 13)	17. False (p. 17)	30. goals (p. 15)
5. True (pp. 13–14)	18. D (p. 13)	31. (No answer, pp. 13–14)
6. False (p. 14)	19. B (p. 13)	32. (No answer, p. 13)
7. True (p. 14)	20. B (p. 13)	33. (No answer, p. 14)
8. False (p. 14)	21. C (pp. 13–14)	34. (No answer, p. 14)
9. False (p. 14)	22. A (p. 14)	35. (No answer, p. 14)
10. True (p. 14)	23. B (p. 14)	36. (No answer, p. 14)
11. True (p. 14)	24. C (p. 14)	37. (No answer, p. 15)
12. True (p. 15)	25. D (p. 14)	38. (No answer, p. 16)
13. True (p. 15)	26. B (p. 15)	39. (No answer, p. 17)

4 Types of Speeches

TRUE/FALSE QUESTIONS

1. Professional speaking is one of the three broad types of speeches.

2. The goal of an informative speech is to increase the audience's understanding or awareness.

3. A persuasive speech should represent at least two viewpoints.

4. A special occasion speech is also called a ceremonial speech.

5. A special occasion speech can also be an informative or persuasive speech.

6. There are three broad types of public speaking.

7. Informative speeches may be about objects, people, events, processes, concepts, or issues.

8. A sample informative speech topic is "The NBA Draft Needs Fixing."

9. Many persuasive speeches focus on perspective taking.

10. One way to determine the type of speech is to look at the goal of the speech.

11. An informative speech is also called a ceremonial speech.

12. A sample persuasive speech topic is "Spay or Neuter Your Pet."

MULTIPLE-CHOICE QUESTIONS

13. Informative speeches may be about
    A) objects. C) people.
    B) events. D) all of the above.

14. Leading the audience to a perspective that is the speaker's is called
    A) informative speaking. C) deception.
    B) perspective taking. D) delivery.

15. The type of speech that is intended to influence the attitudes, beliefs, values, and acts of others is
    A) informative. C) persuasive.
    B) special occasion. D) all of the above.

16. The type of speech that is prepared for a specific occasion and for a purpose dictated by that occasion is
    A) informative.   C) persuasive.
    B) special occasion.   D) all of the above.

17. The type of speech that provides an audience with new information, new insights, or new ways of thinking about a topic is
    A) informative.   C) persuasive.
    B) special occasion.   D) all of the above.

FILL-IN-THE-BLANK QUESTIONS

18. The underlying function of a(n) _____ speech is to entertain, celebrate, commemorate, inspire, or set a social agenda.

19. A eulogy is an example of a(n) _____ speech.

20. A(n) _____ speech provides an audience with new information, new insights, or new ways of thinking about a topic.

21. "The Top Ten Conspiracy Theories" is an example of a(n) _____ speech topic.

22. Speeches about objects, people, events, processes, concepts, or issues are examples of _____ speeches.

23. "The NBA Draft Needs Fixing" is an example of a(n) _____ speech topic.

24. A(n) _____ speech is intended to influence the attitudes, beliefs, values, and acts of others.

ESSAY AND SHORT ANSWER QUESTIONS

25. List the three types of speeches.

26. What is the difference between an informative speech and a persuasive speech?

27. What is the difference between a special occasion speech and an informative speech?

28. What is perspective taking?

29. How can you identify a speech type?

30. Provide examples of an informative speech topic and a persuasive speech topic.

ANSWER KEY FOR CHAPTER 4

1. False (p. 17)
2. True (p. 17)
3. True (p. 18)
4. True (p. 18)
5. True (p. 18)
6. True (p. 17)
7. True (p. 17)
8. False (p. 18)
9. True (p. 18)
10. True (p. 18)

11. False (p. 18)
12. True (p. 18)
13. D (p. 17)
14. B (p. 18)
15. C (p. 18)
16. B (p. 18)
17. A (p. 17)
18. special occasion (p. 19)
19. special occasion (p. 19)
20. informative (p. 17)

21. informative (p. 17)
22. informative (p. 17)
23. persuasive (p. 18)
24. persuasive (p. 18)
25. (No answer, pp. 17–19)
26. (No answer, pp. 17–18)
27. (No answer, pp. 17–19)
28. (No answer, p. 18)
29. (No answer, p. 18)
30. (No answer, pp. 17–18)

From A to Z: Overview of a Speech 5

TRUE/FALSE QUESTIONS

1. The first step in creating a speech involves stating the purpose of the speech.

2. When selecting a speech topic, a speaker should be guided solely by the audience's interests.

3. Audience analysis is a highly systematic process of understanding the audience in relation to the speech topic and the speaking occasion.

4. The general purpose of a speech is usually only to inform the audience.

5. There are two general speech purposes: to inform and to persuade.

6. The specific purpose of a speech is the same as the general purpose.

7. The general purpose of a speech focuses more closely on the goal of the speech than does the specific purpose.

8. A thesis statement is a sentence that clearly expresses the central idea of a speech.

9. A speaker should always use the thesis statement as a guidepost to develop and support the speech's main points.

10. Forming a specific purpose for a speech occurs after you formulate your thesis statement.

11. An effective speech should be organized around four or five main points.

12. Supporting material for a speech lends credibility to the speaker's message.

13. Every speech has three major parts: an introduction, body, and conclusion.

14. An introduction serves to introduce the topic and the speaker and to tell the audience the specific purpose of the speech.

15. During the body of a speech, the speaker should alert the audience to the specific purpose of the speech.

16. The speech body contains the main points and subpoints of the speech.

17. Supporting material is used mostly during the body of the speech.

18. Supporting material should never be used during the introduction of a speech.

19. The conclusion restates the speech purpose and reiterates how the main points confirm it.

20. A speaker should end on a strong note during the conclusion.

21. An outline provides the framework on which to arrange main points in support of the thesis.

22. In a speech outline, coordinate points are given less weight than the main points they support.

23. A speaker should develop either a working outline or a speaking outline, but not both.

24. Presentation aids are always visual.

25. Presentation aids help the audience retain ideas and understand difficult concepts.

26. To deliver an effective speech, a speaker should practice the speech at least five times.

27. The success of a speech depends on the preparation and practice put forth by the speaker.

MULTIPLE-CHOICE QUESTIONS

28. The first step in the speech process is
    A) research.
    B) stating the purpose.
    C) developing points.
    D) selecting a topic.

29. When selecting a speech topic, a speaker should first consider which of the following as a guide?
    A) the time limit
    B) his or her interests
    C) serious issues
    D) historical events

30. The first step in the speechmaking process is _____ ; the last step is _____ .
    A) analyzing the audience; considering presentation aids
    B) selecting a topic; practicing delivery of the speech
    C) stating the speech purpose; outlining the speech
    D) composing a thesis statement; gathering supporting materials

31. The demographic characteristics of an audience include
    A) the ratio of males to females.
    B) racial and ethnic representation.
    C) age variations.
    D) all of the above.

32. Audience analysis involves the study of an audience through techniques such as
    A) interviews and questionnaires.
    B) observation and tape-recording.
    C) surveys and assumptions.
    D) interviews and conjecture.

33. Audience analysis is a highly systematic process of getting to know the listeners relative to
    A) the topic and the speech occasion.
    B) the topic and the time limit.
    C) the speech occasion and the general purpose.
    D) the speech purpose and the time limit.

34. To inform, to persuade, and to mark a special occasion are the three types of
    A) general purposes.   C) thesis statements.
    B) specific purposes.   D) speech occasions.

35. Anne chose to give a speech to her classmates about categories of computer games. The general purpose of Anne's speech was
    A) to inform.   C) to mark a special occasion.
    B) to persuade.   D) none of the above.

The following four phrases pertain to a specific speech. Use the phrases to answer questions 36–38.

Phrase 1: the Department of Transportation (DOT)

Phrase 2: DOT programs available online to serve community members

Phrase 3: to inform

Phrase 4: to inform the audience about three online DOT programs for consumers

— hazardous road conditions, vehicle registration, and driver's license renewals

— so that they will be able to use the services of these programs

36. Which phrase is the narrowed topic?
    A) phrase 1   C) phrase 3
    B) phrase 2   D) phrase 4

37. Which phrase is the general purpose?
    A) phrase 1   C) phrase 3
    B) phrase 2   D) phrase 4

38. Which phrase is the specific purpose?
    A) phrase 1   C) phrase 3
    B) phrase 2   D) phrase 4

39. The _____ is an explicit statement of what you expect your speech to accomplish.
    A) general purpose   C) audience analysis
    B) specific purpose   D) topic selection

40. An effective speech should be organized around _____ main points.
    A) one or two   C) four or five
    B) two or three   D) seven or eight

41. Supporting material illustrates main points by _____ the speaker's main ideas.
    A) substituting   C) verifying
    B) disproving   D) all of the above

42. Which part of a speech sets the tone for the entire speech?
    A) introduction   C) conclusion
    B) body   D) outline

43. In which part of a speech should the speaker illustrate each main point using supporting material?
    A) introduction   C) conclusion
    B) body   D) outline

44. Which part of a speech represents the speaker's last opportunity to motivate listeners and memorably state the theme of the speech?
    A) introduction   C) conclusion
    B) body   D) outline

45. In an outline, what kind of points support the main points?
    A) coordinate   C) equivalent
    B) subordinate   D) superior

46. Which kind of outline is usually brief and contains key words or phrases?
    A) working   C) specific
    B) speaking   D) operational

47. Outlines are based on the principle of
    A) coordination and subordination.
    B) general and specific purpose.
    C) primacy and recency.
    D) topic selection.

48. Presentation aids
    A) summarize and highlight information.
    B) help the audience retain ideas and understand difficult concepts.
    C) provide dramatic emphasis.
    D) can do all of the above.

49. A speech should be practiced at least how many times?
    A) five   C) eight
    B) seven   D) nine

FILL-IN-THE-BLANK QUESTIONS

50. Selecting a topic is the _____ step in preparing a speech.

51. The process of _____ helps to determine how receptive the audience will be toward a given topic.

52. To inform, to persuade, to entertain, and to mark a special occasion are general speech _____ .

53. After a speaker has identified the general and specific purposes of the speech, he or she should then write a concise _____ statement that identifies what the speech is about.

54. Newspaper editorials, Internet sites, and pictures are examples of places to locate _____ for a speech.

55. The introduction, body, and conclusion make up the three parts of a(n) _____ .

56. The part of a speech that contains the main ideas and supporting material is the _____ .

57. In an outline, _____ points are of equal importance and are indicated by their parallel alignment.

ESSAY AND SHORT ANSWER QUESTIONS

58. List two ways in which a speaker can select a topic.

59. How can a speaker analyze the audience?

60. Why is it important to identify the purpose of a speech?

61. What are the components of a good thesis statement?

62. Why should a speech be separated into its major parts?

63. Identify the functions of the introduction, the body, and the conclusion.

64. Explain the difference between a working outline and a speaking outline.

65. How do presentation aids benefit a speech?

66. Discuss the importance of practicing a speech.

ANSWER KEY FOR CHAPTER 5

1. False (p. 20)	23. False (p. 23)	45. B (p. 23)
2. False (p. 20)	24. False (p. 24)	46. B (pp. 23–24)
3. True (p. 20)	25. True (p. 24)	47. A (p. 23)
4. False (p. 20)	26. True (p. 24)	48. D (p. 24)
5. False (p. 20)	27. True (p. 24)	49. A (p. 24)
6. False (p. 20)	28. D (p. 20)	50. first (p. 20)
7. False (p. 20)	29. B (p. 20)	51. audience analysis (p. 20)
8. True (p. 21)	30. B (p. 19)	52. purposes (p. 20)
9. True (p. 21)	31. D (p. 20)	53. thesis (p. 21)
10. False (pp. 20–21)	32. A (p. 20)	54. supporting material (p. 22)
11. False (p. 21)	33. A (p. 20)	55. speech (p. 22)
12. True (p. 22)	34. A (p. 20)	56. body (p. 23)
13. True (p. 22)	35. A (p. 20)	57. coordinate (p. 23)
14. True (p. 22)	36. B (pp. 20–21)	58. (No answer, p. 20)
15. False (p. 22)	37. C (pp. 20–21)	59. (No answer, p. 20)
16. True (p. 23)	38. D (pp. 20–21)	60. (No answer, p. 20)
17. True (p. 23)	39. B (p. 20)	61. (No answer, p. 21)
18. False (p. 23)	40. B (p. 21)	62. (No answer, p. 22)
19. True (p. 23)	41. C (p. 22)	63. (No answer, pp. 22–23)
20. True (p. 23)	42. A (p. 22)	64. (No answer, pp. 23–24)
21. True (p. 23)	43. B (p. 23)	65. (No answer, p. 24)
22. False (p. 23)	44. C (p. 23)	66. (No answer, p. 24)

6 *Managing Speech Anxiety*

TRUE/FALSE QUESTIONS

1. When properly channeled, a speaker's nervousness can boost his or her performance.

2. PSA (public-speaking anxiety) is a speaker's fear or anxiety associated with either actual or anticipated communication to an audience.

3. Lack of experience does not generally increase a speaker's public-speaking anxiety.

4. Feeling different from audience members is common among public speakers.

5. When speakers focus on themselves, they become less sensitive to things that might be wrong with their performance.

6. The onset of public-speaking anxiety can occur at different times during the speechmaking process.

7. Pre-preparation anxiety usually occurs when a speaker rehearses the speech.

8. Performance anxiety in speechmaking is usually most pronounced as the speech builds to its climax.

9. Gaining confidence in public speaking comes about through preparation and practice.

10. Having a positive attitude toward speechmaking results in a raised heart rate during the delivery of a speech.

11. Thinking of public speaking as a threat can be part of positive thinking about public speaking, since such thoughts give speakers an edge.

12. Thinking about your speech from a "communication orientation" will give you a more positive outlook on your public speaking experience.

13. Visualization is not an effective technique for building speaker confidence.

14. When you feel stressed, the center of your breathing tends to move from the upper chest to the back of the throat, leaving you with a reduced supply of air.

15. In stress-control breathing, the center of breathing is felt in the back of the throat.

16. Stage one of stress-control breathing involves using a calming word in a mantra.

17. Practicing natural gestures is a relaxation technique.

18. The most effective speakers stand perfectly still behind a podium and do not walk around.

19. A speaker's movement serves to relieve tension and helps to hold the audience's attention.

20. Giving a speech can be a satisfying and empowering experience.

MULTIPLE-CHOICE QUESTIONS

21. Feeling _____ is one reason many people are uncomfortable about public speaking.
    A) attractive
    B) superior to the audience
    C) different
    D) depersonalized

22. A speaker's general fear or anxiety associated with either actual or anticipated communication to an audience is known as
    A) communication nervousness.
    B) communication uneasiness.
    C) public-speaking anxiety.
    D) stage fright.

23. Feeling different when delivering a speech
    A) does not bother most public speakers.
    B) is common among politicians.
    C) makes a speaker feel anxious about being the center of attention.
    D) is none of the above.

24. Tyson began to panic as soon as his instructor gave the speech assignment to the class. Tyson experienced
    A) pre-preparation anxiety.
    B) preparation anxiety.
    C) pre-performance anxiety.
    D) performance anxiety.

25. Claire began to feel nervous once she began organizing and writing her speech. Which type of anxiety did Claire experience?
    A) pre-preparation anxiety
    B) preparation anxiety
    C) pre-performance anxiety
    D) performance anxiety

26. Each of the following is a successful strategy for gaining public-speaking confidence *except*
    A) modifying thoughts and attitudes.
    B) personalizing the speech evaluation.
    C) seeking pleasure in the occasion.
    D) practicing the speech.

FILL-IN-THE-BLANK QUESTIONS

27. Feeling different from the audience, a lack of public-speaking experience, and uneasiness about being the center of attention can lead to _____.

28. Katarina experienced _____ anxiety as soon as she realized she had to give a speech.

29. The onset of nervousness that occurs during the rehearsal of a speech is called _____ anxiety.

30. The type of anxiety that is most pronounced during the introduction phase of a speech is termed _____ anxiety.

31. As Bizhi prepared to give her speech, she mentally pictured herself giving a successful speech. To build confidence, Bizhi was practicing _____.

32. A form of breathing in which the center of breathing is felt in the stomach rather than in the chest is called _____ breathing.

ESSAY AND SHORT ANSWER QUESTIONS

33. Describe some ways a speaker feels different when presenting a speech.

34. Explain why public speaking is such a source of anxiety for most people.

35. Explain how being the center of attention can contribute to an uncomfortable speech situation.

36. Identify the type of public-speaking anxiety that affects you most, and describe how you cope with it.

37. List two times when anxiety can occur in the speechmaking process.

38. How can speakers increase their confidence by changing their thinking about public speaking from a "performance orientation" to a "communication orientation"?

39. Write a brief account of how you can use visualization to build public-speaking confidence.

ANSWER KEY FOR CHAPTER 6

1. True (p. 25)	14. False (p. 30)	27. public-speaking anxiety (p. 25)
2. True (p. 25)	15. False (pp. 30–31)	28. pre-preparation (p. 27)
3. False (p. 25)	16. False (p. 30)	29. pre-performance (p. 28)
4. True (p. 26)	17. True (p. 31)	30. performance (p. 28)
5. False (p. 26)	18. False (p. 31)	31. visualization (p. 29)
6. True (p. 27)	19. True (p. 31)	32. stress-control (p. 30)
7. False (p. 27)	20. True (p. 32)	33. (No answer, p. 26)
8. False (p. 28)	21. C (p. 26)	34. (No answer, pp. 25–26)
9. True (p. 29)	22. C (p. 25)	35. (No answer, p. 26)
10. False (p. 29)	23. C (p. 26)	36. (No answer, pp. 27–28)
11. False (p. 29)	24. A (p. 27)	37. (No answer, pp. 27–28)
12. True (p. 29)	25. B (p. 27)	38. (No answer, p. 29)
13. False (p. 29)	26. B (pp. 28–32)	39. (No answer, pp. 29–30)

7 Analyzing the Audience

TRUE/FALSE QUESTIONS

1. Audience analysis is the process of gathering and analyzing information about listeners.

2. It is important for a speaker to understand an audience's beliefs and attitudes, but not their values.

3. Beliefs reflect a predisposition to respond to people, ideas, objects, or events in evaluative ways.

4. Values are based on attitudes.

5. Beliefs are shaped by values.

6. People's most enduring judgments about what is good and bad in life are called *attitudes*.

7. A speaker should try to uncover the audience's feelings toward the speech topic, the speaker, and the speech occasion.

8. As a general rule, people give more interest and attention to topics about which they have a negative attitude.

9. An audience that holds negative attitudes toward the speaker will tend to disregard even the most important or interesting message.

10. All audience members bring the same set of expectations and emotions to a speech event.

11. If audience members are negatively disposed toward your topic, as a speaker you should provide them with good reasons for why their attitudes are unfounded.

12. Demographics are the psychological characteristics of a given population.

13. Speech topics should be relevant to the age interests of an audience.

14. Gender is not a demographic characteristic.

15. The term *cultural patterns* refers to oversimplified and distorted ideas about the innate nature of men or women.

16. Thinking of females as nurturers and caregivers is an example of a gender stereotype.

17. The cultural patterns of behavior identified by Hofstede are called *value dimensions.*

18. Collectivist cultures view personal identity, needs, and desires as secondary to those of the larger group.

19. Cultures with high levels of power distance place greater value on social equality.

20. *Uncertainty avoidance* refers to the extent to which people feel threatened by ambiguity.

21. Traditional feminine traits include ambition and earning power.

22. Culture influences our values.

23. The dominant values in the United States rank higher in masculinity than in femininity.

24. Venezuela, Peru, and Taiwan rank highest in individualistic characteristics.

25. Socioeconomic status includes income, occupation, and education.

26. Income is a demographic factor that does not pervasively affect people's life experiences.

27. Occupational interests are tied to politics, the economy, education, and social reform.

28. Generally, the level of education a person has influences his/her ideas and perspectives.

29. Being aware of an audience's general religious orientation can help a speaker know how the audience will respond to controversial topics.

30. Political issues are not usually touchy subjects for most audiences.

31. Interviews and surveys are the only methods of audience analysis.

32. For audience analysis, interviews generally take less time to implement than do surveys.

33. In a survey questionnaire, fixed alternative questions measure the respondent's level of agreement or disagreement with specific issues.

34. Published sources are helpful in conducting audience analysis.

35. The physical setting in which a speech occurs can have a significant impact on the outcome of a speech.

36. It is not usually helpful to a speaker to know the audience's seating arrangement.

MULTIPLE-CHOICE QUESTIONS

37. Which of the following would be considered an attitude rather than a belief or a value?
    A) "I believe in God."   C) "Honesty is essential to friendship."
    B) "I like rap music."   D) "Life should be financially secure."

38. Values are
    A) our conceptions of what is true and false.
    B) our predispositions to respond to things in evaluative ways.
    C) our perceptions of reality.
    D) our most enduring judgments about what is good and bad in life.

39. A speaker should try to uncover the audience's feelings toward
    A) the speech topic.   C) the speech occasion.
    B) the speaker.   D) all of the above.

40. Which of the following would *not* be considered a demographic characteristic?
    A) gender   C) self-esteem
    B) ethnic or cultural background   D) religion

41. The statistical characteristics of a given population or group of people are known as
    A) psychographics.   C) profiles.
    B) demographics.   D) beliefs.

42. How many demographic characteristics are typically considered in the analysis of speech audiences?
    A) three   C) five
    B) four   D) six

43. Which of the following countries does *not* rank high on individualism?
    A) Venezuela   C) Great Britain
    B) Australia   D) Canada

44. Which cultures structure life more rigidly and formally for their members?
    A) low-uncertainty avoidance cultures
    B) high-uncertainty avoidance cultures
    C) low power distance cultures
    D) high masculine cultures

45. Sweden, Norway, Finland, and Denmark are the countries ranking highest in
    A) low-uncertainty avoidance.   C) femininity.
    B) high power distance   D) none of the above.

46. Socioeconomic status (SES) includes
    A) gender, occupation, and religion.
    B) ethnicity, education, and occupation.
    C) income, occupation, and education.
    D) none of the above.

47. Tools a speaker can use to analyze an audience include
    A) interviews.   C) published sources.
    B) surveys.   D) all of the above.

48. If you ask survey respondents to respond to questions with a limited choice of
    answers, you are asking what type of questions?
    A) interview   C) scale
    B) fixed alternative   D) open-ended

49. _____ allow a mix of open-ended and closed-ended questions.
    A) Interviews   C) Both A and B
    B) Surveys   D) Written sources

50. In an interview, what type of questions are particularly useful for probing beliefs
    and opinions?
    A) closed-ended   C) scale
    B) fixed alternative   D) open-ended

51. Interview questions that invite elaboration are _____ questions.
    A) open-ended   C) confidential
    B) closed-ended   D) scale

52. Which type of questions on a survey may be either fixed-alternative or scale
    questions?
    A) open-ended   C) analytical
    B) closed-ended   D) potential

53. Characteristics of the speech setting include
    A) the size of the audience and the length of the speech.
    B) lighting and sound.
    C) seating capacity and arrangement.
    D) all of the above.

FILL-IN-THE-BLANK QUESTIONS

54. Audience analysis is the process by which a speaker discovers the needs and interests of a particular audience regarding the speech _____ .

55. _____ stereotypes are oversimplified and often distorted ideas about the innate nature of men or women.

56. Interviews and surveys are appropriate tools for audience _____ .

57. A(n) _____ is a form of face-to-face communication for the purpose of gathering information.

58. Questions that seek no particular response and allow respondents to elaborate as much as they wish are known as _____ questions.

59. Questions that measure the respondent's level of agreement or disagreement with particular issues are called _____ questions.

60. Location, time, seating arrangements, light, and sound are all components of the physical speech _____ .

ESSAY AND SHORT ANSWER QUESTIONS

61. Explain the relationship among attitudes, beliefs, and values.

62. Why are audience demographics an important source of information for a speaker?

63. Using your own experience, discuss an example of a gender stereotype.

64. Define socioeconomic status (SES) and explain its importance in the process of audience analysis.

65. Use an example to explain how religion can be a powerful predictor of audience response.

66. Identify the thesis statement for your last (or next) speech. Then imagine that you are conducting a survey on this speech topic. List four fixed-alternative survey questions that would be appropriate for your speech, audience, and topic.

67. Identify the thesis statement for your last (or next) speech. Then imagine that you are conducting a survey on this speech topic. List four scale survey questions that would be appropriate for your speech, audience, and topic.

68. Provide two examples of an open-ended interview question.

69. Why should a speaker spend time becoming familiar with the speech setting before giving a speech?

70. Discuss how the seating arrangement can affect a speaker's audience.

ANSWER KEY FOR CHAPTER 7

1. True (p. 34)	25. True (p. 36)	49. C (pp. 41–43)
2. False (p. 34)	26. False (p. 37)	50. D (p. 41)
3. False (p. 34)	27. True (p. 37)	51. A (p. 41)
4. False (p. 34)	28. True (p. 37)	52. B (p. 41)
5. True (p. 34)	29. True (p. 37)	53. D (p. 44)
6. False (p. 34)	30. False (p. 38)	54. topic (p. 34)
7. True (p. 34)	31. False (p. 41)	55. Gender (p. 38)
8. False (p. 35)	32. False (p. 41)	56. analysis (p. 41)
9. True (p. 35)	33. False (p. 41)	57. interview (p. 42)
10. False (p. 35)	34. True (pp. 43–44)	58. open-ended (p. 41)
11. True (p. 35)	35. True (p. 44)	59. scale (p. 41)
12. False (p. 36)	36. False (p. 44)	60. setting (p. 44)
13. True (p. 36)	37. B (p. 34)	61. (No answer, p. 34)
14. False (p. 38)	38. D (p. 34)	62. (No answer, p. 36)
15. False (p. 38)	39. D (p. 34)	63. (No answer, p. 38)
16. True (p. 38)	40. C (pp. 36–37)	64. (No answer, pp. 36–37)
17. True (p. 38)	41. B (p. 36)	65. (No answer, p. 37)
18. True (p. 39)	42. D (p. 36)	66. (No answer, p. 41)
19. False (p. 39)	43. A (p. 39)	67. (No answer, p. 41)
20. True (p. 39)	44. B (p. 39)	68. (No answer, p. 41)
21. False (p. 40)	45. C (p. 39)	69. (No answer, p. 44)
22. True (p. 38)	46. C (p. 36)	70. (No answer, p. 44)
23. True (p. 40)	47. D (pp. 41–44)	
24. False (p. 39)	48. B (p. 41)	

Selecting a Topic and Purpose *8*

TRUE/FALSE QUESTIONS

1. As long as your speech topic interests you, it will be appropriate to the audience and occasion.

2. When a speaker chooses a speech topic, he or she is not held accountable for accomplishing a particular purpose.

3. The three general speech purposes are to inform, to persuade, and to entertain.

4. When selecting a topic for an informative speech, the speaker should try to gauge what the audience already knows about the topic.

5. Speaking over or under audience members' heads does not affect their attention to a speech.

6. If the audience is familiar with a speech topic, the speaker should attempt to present the knowledge in a fresh and interesting way.

7. To develop an interesting speech, a speaker should choose a topic with which he or she is unfamiliar.

8. Current events are generally considered boring choices for speech topics.

9. Grassroots issues are interesting topic choices for speakers.

10. Brainstorming is a problem-solving technique involving the spontaneous generation of ideas.

11. To narrow a speech topic, you need to consider time constraints, audience expectations, and the nature of the occasion.

12. Brainstorming is not an effective way to narrow a speech topic.

13. The specific speech purpose focuses more closely on the speech's goal than does the general speech purpose.

14. Speech topic choices should always be guided by ethical considerations.

15. The thesis statement is the theme or central idea of the speech.

16. If a speech is informative, its thesis statement does not propose that claims made are true or believed.

17. A well-written thesis statement aids the speaker in developing a coherent, understandable speech.

18. A thesis statement should always be entertaining and clever.

MULTIPLE-CHOICE QUESTIONS

19. Speech topics may be
    A) assigned.
    B) self-selected.
    C) either A or B.
    D) neither A nor B.

20. The _____ speech purpose answers the question, "Why am I speaking on this topic for this particular audience and occasion?"
    A) general
    B) specific
    C) informative
    D) persuasive

21. The purpose of a(n) _____ speech is to increase the audience's understanding and awareness of a topic.
    A) commemorative
    B) persuasive
    C) informative
    D) challenge

22. Personal interests for a speech topic include
    A) favorite activities and hobbies.
    B) goals and values.
    C) both A and B.
    D) neither A nor B.

23. Grassroots issues are
    A) poor speech topic choices.
    B) issues that don't affect the audience directly.
    C) usually local in nature.
    D) both B and C.

24. When narrowing a topic, the speaker should consider
    A) the time limit for speaking.
    B) the speech purpose.
    C) the amount of time available for research.
    D) all of the above.

25. The _____ speech purpose expresses both the topic and the general speech purpose in action form and identifies the speaker's specific objectives.
    A) general
    B) initial
    C) specific
    D) ethical

FILL-IN-THE-BLANK QUESTIONS

26. To inform, to persuade, and to mark a special occasion are the three general speech _____ .

27. A(n) _____ speech describes, defines, explains, or demonstrates something.

28. The general purpose of a(n) _____ speech is to effect some degree of change in the audience.

29. If a speaker selects a topic that he or she is enthusiastic about and familiar with, the topic choice is based on _____ interests.

30. The problem-solving technique involving the spontaneous generation of ideas is termed _____ .

31. When you _____ a speech topic, you focus on specific aspects of it, to the exclusion of others.

32. The _____ statement is the theme or central idea of the speech.

ESSAY AND SHORT ANSWER QUESTIONS

33. How does the general speech purpose differ from the specific speech purpose?

34. List three topics suitable for a persuasive speech.

35. If you were assigned to write a speech based on your personal interests, what four topics would you consider for your speech?

36. Identify two current events or controversial issues appropriate for a classroom speech.

37. Identify two contemporary grassroots issues appropriate for a classroom speech.

38. Discuss three things to consider when narrowing a speech topic.

39. Describe the components of the specific speech purpose.

40. Describe the similarities and differences between the thesis statement and the specific speech purpose.

41. Explain why the nature of the thesis statement varies according to the speech purpose.

42. Choose a speech topic. Then write (a) a general speech purpose, (b) a specific speech purpose, and (c) a thesis statement.

43. How can a speaker make a thesis statement relevant to and motivating for the audience?

ANSWER KEY FOR CHAPTER 8

1. False (p. 45)
2. False (p. 45)
3. False (p. 45)
4. True (p. 47)
5. False (p. 45)
6. True (p. 45)
7. False (p. 45)
8. False (p. 46)
9. True (p. 45)
10. True (p. 47)
11. True (p. 47)
12. False (p. 47)
13. True (p. 48)
14. False (p. 46)
15. True (pp. 48–49)

16. False (p. 49)
17. True (p. 50)
18. False (p. 50)
19. C (p. 45)
20. A (p. 45)
21. C (p. 45)
22. C (p. 45)
23. C (p. 45)
24. D (pp. 47–48)
25. C (p. 48)
26. purposes (p. 45)
27. informative (p. 45)
28. persuasive (p. 45)
29. personal (p. 45)
30. brainstorming (p. 47)

31. narrow (p. 47)
32. thesis (p. 48)
33. (No answer, pp. 45, 48)
34. (No answer, p. 45)
35. (No answer, p. 45)
36. (No answer, p. 46)
37. (No answer, p. 46)
38. (No answer, p. 47)
39. (No answer, p. 48)
40. (No answer, p. 49)
41. (No answer, p. 49)
42. (No answer, pp. 45, 48–49)
43. (No answer, p. 49)

Developing Supporting Material **9**

TRUE/FALSE QUESTIONS

1. Examples in a speech weaken understanding by making ideas, items, or events less concrete.

2. Examples in a speech can be brief or extended.

3. One of the most powerful means of conveying a message is through a narrative, or story.

4. Hypothetical examples are effective for making a point about something that has already occurred.

5. Narratives tell tales that are either real or imaginary.

6. Testimony comprises firsthand findings, eyewitness accounts, and opinions.

7. Lay testimony is testimony by nonexperts.

8. Most people require some type of evidence before they will accept a speaker's position or claims.

9. Facts are summarized data that demonstrate trends or show relationships.

10. Inferential statistics represent only the people or places they reference.

11. Inferential statistics are data collected from a sample or representative group and then generalized to a larger population.

12. In evaluating facts and statistics as supporting material for a speech, it is important to determine whether the source is credible.

MULTIPLE-CHOICE QUESTIONS

13. When used as supporting material in a speech, examples can
    A) illustrate.   C) clarify.
    B) describe.   D) do all of the above.

14. Effective examples for a speech may be all of the following except
    A) hypothetical.   C) factual.
    B) extended.   D) extraneous.

15. Which type of example offers a single illustration of a point?
    A) brief
    B) extended
    C) factual
    D) hypothetical

16. Which type of example offers a multifaceted illustration of a point?
    A) brief
    B) extended
    C) factual
    D) hypothetical

17. Legends, fairy tales, myths, and other stories are considered
    A) perspectives.
    B) narratives.
    C) testimonies.
    D) statistics.

18. A plot, characters, setting, and a time line are all essential to
    A) contextual examples.
    B) extended examples.
    C) storytelling.
    D) credibility.

19. Brief stories of interesting, humorous, or real-life incidents are called
    A) facts.
    B) testimony.
    C) statistics.
    D) anecdotes.

20. If a medical doctor gives cutting-edge information on the threat of high cholesterol, she is providing which type of supporting material?
    A) narrative material
    B) lay testimony
    C) expert testimony
    D) all of the above

21. The credibility of testimony can be evaluated by checking
    A) the reliability of the source.
    B) the timeliness of the information.
    C) both A and B.
    D) neither A nor B.

22. When citing testimony in a speech, the speaker should always
    A) supply the name and qualifications of the source.
    B) supply the inferential statistics related to the source.
    C) provide information about when, but not where, the testimony was offered.
    D) do none of the above.

23. Which type of statistic is useful for making predictions?
    A) descriptive
    B) expert
    C) inferential
    D) factual

24. Which type of statistic requires that the data must come from a representative sample?
    A) descriptive
    B) expert
    C) inferential
    D) factual

FILL-IN-THE-BLANK QUESTIONS

25. _____ are a type of supporting material that aids audience understanding by making ideas, items, or events more concrete.

26. _____ , which aid audience understanding, can be brief or extended and either factual or hypothetical.

27. _____ examples are effective for making a point about something that could happen in the future.

28. _____ , or stories, tell tales that are either real or imaginary.

29. Brief stories of interesting, humorous, or real-life incidents are called _____ .

30. Firsthand findings, eyewitness accounts, and opinions are types of _____ .

31. _____ testimony includes findings, eyewitness accounts, or opinions by professionals who are qualified on a particular subject.

32. _____ testimony is testimony by nonexperts.

33. Documented occurrences, including actual events, dates, times, people involved, and places, are known as _____ .

34. _____ are used to express data in numerical form.

35. Summarized data that demonstrate trends or show relationships are known as _____ .

36. _____ statistics represent only the people or places they reference.

37. _____ statistics are data collected from a sample or representative group and then generalized to a larger population.

ESSAY AND SHORT ANSWER QUESTIONS

38. Provide an extended example for the topic "weight loss."

39. Why is a narrative such a powerful and compelling type of supporting material?

40. Explain why personal experiences make good narratives.

41. What is the difference between expert testimony and lay testimony?

42. How do facts differ from statistics?

43. When are statistics effective as supporting material in a speech?

44. Compare and contrast descriptive and inferential statistics.

45. List three criteria for evaluating facts and statistics.

ANSWER KEY FOR CHAPTER 9

1. False (p. 51)	16. B (pp. 51–52)	31. Expert (p. 54)
2. True (pp. 51–52)	17. B (p. 52)	32. Lay (p. 54)
3. True (p. 52)	18. C (p. 52)	33. facts (p. 54)
4. False (p. 52)	19. D (p. 53)	34. Statistics (p. 54)
5. True (p. 52)	20. C (p. 54)	35. statistics (p. 54)
6. True (p. 54)	21. C (p. 54)	36. Descriptive (p. 54)
7. True (p. 54)	22. A (p. 54)	37. Inferential (p. 55)
8. True (p. 54)	23. C (pp. 54–55)	38. (No answer, p. 52)
9. False (p. 54)	24. C (pp. 54–55)	39. (No answer, p. 52)
10. False (p. 55)	25. Examples (pp. 51–52)	40. (No answer, p. 53)
11. True (p. 55)	26. Examples (pp. 51–52)	41. (No answer, p. 54)
12. True (p. 55)	27. Hypothetical (p. 52)	42. (No answer, p. 54)
13. D (p. 51)	28. Narratives (p. 52)	43. (No answer, p. 55)
14. D (pp. 51–52)	29. anecdotes (p. 53)	44. (No answer, pp. 54–55)
15. A (pp. 51–52)	30. testimony (p. 54)	45. (No answer, pp. 55–56)

10 *Locating Supporting Material*

1. Supporting material drawn from secondary research can include any source developed directly by the participants involved.

2. Original or firsthand research conducted by the speaker is primary research.

3. Two types of primary research are interviews and surveys.

4. Information recorded by individuals other than actual participants in an event or study is termed secondary research.

5. Books explore topics superficially, not in depth.

6. A regularly published magazine or journal is called a periodical.

7. Some periodical databases are devoted to special topics.

8. GPO publications are not good sources for government documents and statistics.

9. Encyclopedias, almanacs, and atlases are examples of reference works.

10. General encyclopedias delve deeply into one subject area.

11. The *Encyclopedia Britannica* is an example of a specialized encyclopedia.

12. Almanacs may be general or specialized.

13. Almanacs and fact books are good places to find facts and statistics in support of a speech topic.

14. Biographical resources contain information about famous or noteworthy people.

15. Books of quotations and poetry collections are not examples of reference works.

16. An atlas is a collection of maps and text accompanied by charts and tables.

17. Multicultural reference works are unavailable to researchers.

18. To assess the credibility of a publication, the speaker should check out the publisher and determine whether the source is reputable.

MULTIPLE-CHOICE QUESTIONS

19. The vast world of information gathered by others is called _____ research.
    A) primary   C) tertiary
    B) secondary   D) questionnaire

20. Which of the following are types of primary research?
    A) interviews and personal observations
    B) almanacs
    C) data on CD-ROMs
    D) all of the above

21. Primary research does not include
    A) information gathered by others.   C) personal surveys.
    B) personal interviews.   D) all of the above.

22. *US News & World Report, Newsweek,* and *Time* are examples of
    A) government publications.   C) almanacs.
    B) periodicals.   D) biographical resources.

23. The *Guide to U.S. Government Publications* is available
    A) in print.   C) online.
    B) on microfiche.   D) in all of the above forms.

24. Which type of reference work summarizes knowledge that is found in original form elsewhere?
    A) encyclopedias   C) biographical resources
    B) almanacs   D) poetry collections

25. A regularly published magazine or journal is called a(n)
    A) annual.   C) periodical.
    B) yearbook.   D) guide.

26. The *Biography Index* indexes biographical material from
    A) periodicals, books, and obituaries.
    B) only periodicals.
    C) almanacs, periodicals, and obituaries.
    D) none of the above.

27. Material from books of _____ is often used by speakers in introductions and conclusions.
    A) myths   C) history
    B) quotations   D) biography

28. An example of a multicultural reference work is
    A) the *Dictionary of American Biography.*
    B) the *Asian American Almanac.*
    C) both A and B.
    D) neither A nor B.

FILL-IN-THE-BLANK QUESTIONS

29. Information or research gathered by others is called _____ research.

30. A regularly published magazine or journal is called a(n) _____ .

31. Encyclopedias, almanacs, and atlases are examples of _____ works.

32. Encyclopedias that delve deeply into one subject area are known as _____ encyclopedias.

33. The *Encyclopedia Britannica* is an example of a(n) _____ encyclopedia.

34. A collection of maps and text accompanied by charts and tables is called a(n) _____ .

ESSAY AND SHORT ANSWER QUESTIONS

35. Explain the difference between primary and secondary research.

36. When you are preparing a speech, why might books be valuable as supporting material?

37. How are newspapers and periodicals more beneficial than books?

38. Describe a speech in which a citation from a government publication would be useful.

39. Explain why books of quotations and poetry collections are good sources for introductions and conclusions to speeches.

40. Provide an example of a speech topic for which a speaker might consult an atlas.

ANSWER KEY FOR CHAPTER 10

1. False (p. 56)
2. True (p. 56)
3. True (p. 56)
4. True (p. 56)
5. False (p. 57)
6. True (p. 57)
7. True (p. 57)
8. False (p. 57)
9. True (p. 58)
10. False (p. 58)
11. False (p. 58)
12. True (p. 58)
13. True (p. 58)
14. True (p. 58)

15. False (p. 59)
16. True (p. 59)
17. False (p. 59)
18. True (p. 60)
19. B (p. 56)
20. A (p. 56)
21. A (p. 56)
22. B (p. 57)
23. D (p. 57)
24. A (p. 58)
25. C (p. 57)
26. A (p. 58)
27. B (pp. 58–59)
28. B (p. 59)

29. secondary (p. 56)
30. periodical (p. 57)
31. reference (p. 58)
32. specialized (p. 58)
33. general (p. 58)
34. atlas (p. 59)
35. (No answer, p. 56)
36. (No answer, p. 58)
37. (No answer, pp. 57–58)
38. (No answer, p. 57)
39. (No answer, pp. 58–59)
40. (No answer, p. 59)

11 *Doing Effective Internet Research*

TRUE/FALSE QUESTIONS

1. The terms *misinformation* and *disinformation* are synonomous.

2. All Internet search engines use the same criteria to determine search relevance.

3. Two types of search engines are individual and meta-search.

4. Pay-for-placement search engines scan a variety of individual search engines simultaneously.

5. MetaCrawler and Dogpile are examples of meta-search engines.

6. Most search engines do not order search results according to relevance.

7. The purpose of propaganda is to instill a particular attitude.

8. Like some search engines, subject directories compile databases of their own.

9. Subject directories can be searched by using keywords or phrases.

10. Both search engines and subject directories offer valuable help in locating supporting materials for a speech.

11. The word *misinformation* always refers to something that is not true.

12. Subject directories are not useful for finding and narrowing a speech topic.

13. Most universities and city libraries offer library gateways in the form of their library's home page.

14. A library's home page will generally contain links to online databases that provide indexing, abstracting, or full-text access to research materials outside the library.

15. A password is not usually required to access databases on a library gateway.

16. Virtual libraries exist on the Internet.

17. The invisible Web is the portion of the Web that includes pass-protected sites, documents behind firewalls, and the contents of proprietary databases.

18. Library gateways and specialty search engines are not good sources of direct links to the invisible Web.

19. Meaningful speeches are based on sound information rather than on misinformation.

20. Kirk's four distinctions to consider when evaluating Internet sources include information, propaganda, misinformation, and periodicals.

21. Information, propaganda, misinformation, and disinformation are four criteria to consider when evaluating Internet sources.

22. A subject directory is a good place to start brainstorming for information on a speech topic.

23. When you use search tools on the Internet, quotation marks help you locate exact phrases.

24. Boolean operators are words placed between keywords in a search that specify how the keywords are related.

25. Using the word OR in an Internet search restricts the search by excluding specific terms from the results.

26. The plus and minus signs are the equivalent of the Boolean operators AND and NOT.

27. One way to evaluate the credibility of a Web site is to look for the last date the site was modified or updated.

28. The domain of a Web address is the suffix at the end of the address that indicates the nature of the site.

29. A tilde (~) in a Web address usually indicates that it is a commerical page.

30. The mission statement or "About Us" link usually tells a great deal about the nature of a particular Web site.

MULTIPLE-CHOICE QUESTIONS

31. The key to a productive search in cyberspace is in
    A) a well-prepared research strategy.
    B) an understanding of the information available on the Internet.
    C) a basic grasp of how to use Internet search tools.
    D) all of the above.

32. To efficiently locate information on the Internet for a speech, the speaker should be familiar with the function of
    A) search engines and subject directories.
    B) library gateways and specialized databases.
    C) both A and B.
    D) neither A nor B.

33. Which of the following is an example of a search engine on the Internet?
    A) AltaVista
    B) Google
    C) Teoma
    D) all of the above

34. Which types of search engines are devoted entirely to one topic?
    A) specialized search engines
    B) subject directories
    C) meta-search engines
    D) individual search engines

35. Which of the following is *not* an important distinction to consider when evaluating Internet sources?
    A) misinformation
    B) propaganda
    C) information
    D) reification

36. _____ refers to something that is not true.
    A) Information
    B) Misinformation
    C) Propaganda
    D) Disinformation

37. A subject directory
    A) is also known as a human directory.
    B) is a searchable database of Web sites submitted to that directory and assigned categories by a human editor.
    C) does not compile databases of its own.
    D) is all of the above.

38. The most effective way to find and narrow a topic online is to use
    A) search engines.
    B) subject directories.
    C) neither A nor B.
    D) both A and B.

39. A subject directory that contains at least 100 sites that have been reviewed by an expert is called a
    A) library catalog.
    B) gateway.
    C) human directory.
    D) search engine.

40. This type of search engine allows advertisers to bid on popular search terms that are relevant to their site, with the top position going to the highest bidder.
    A) crawler-based
    B) pay for placement
    C) individual
    D) specialized

41. The portion of the Web that includes pass-protected sites, documents behind firewalls, and the contents of proprietary databases is called the
    A) imperceptible Web.   C) undetectable Web.
    B) unseen Web.   D) invisible Web.

42. Another name for a *human directory* is
    A) a library portal.   C) a human search.
    B) a subject directory.   D) Commstar.

43. If a speaker is brainstorming ideas online and wants to survey what is available on a particular speech topic, she or he should begin by selecting a
    A) library catalog.   C) subject directory.
    B) gateway.   D) search engine.

44. AND, OR, and NOT are examples of
    A) bookmark tools.   C) domains.
    B) Boolean operators.   D) library gateways.

45. Which of the following words expands an online search?
    A) AND   C) NOT
    B) OR   D) PLUS

46. In an online search, the plus (+) and minus (–) signs are equivalent to the Boolean operator(s)
    A) AND.   C) PLUS and NOT.
    B) OR.   D) AND and NOT.

47. Which of the following domain suffixes indicates a nonprofit group?
    A) .org   C) .com
    B) .net   D) .gov

FILL-IN-THE-BLANK QUESTIONS

48. Search engines that scan individual search engines simultaneously but do not compile their own databases are known as _____ engines.

49. Most search engines rank search results according to _____ .

50. _____ directories are useful for finding and narrowing a speech topic.

51. A(n) _____ is usually required for access to databases on a library gateway.

52. Libraries that exist only on the Internet are known as _____ libraries.

53. The _____ Web is the portion of the Web that includes pass-protected sites, documents behind firewalls, and the contents of proprietary databases.

54. A(n) _____ directory is a good place to start brainstorming for information on a speech topic.

55. _____ are words placed between keywords in a search that specify how the keywords are related.

56. The minus sign is the equivalent of the Boolean operator _____ .

57. The _____ of a Web address is the suffix at the end of the address that indicates the nature of the site.

58. A(n) _____ , or (~), in a Web address usually indicates that it is a personal page.

59. A(n) _____ directory is a searchable database of Web sites that have been submitted to that directory and then assigned by an editor to an appropriate category or categories.

ESSAY AND SHORT ANSWER QUESTIONS

60. Discuss the four important distinctions to consider when evaluating Internet sources.

61. Explain the difference between an individual search engine and a meta-search engine.

62. Describe and provide an example of a specialized search engine.

63. Define *subject directory* and explain its use.

64. When is a subject directory more beneficial to research than a search engine?

65. What is the invisible Web?

66. Describe the steps in creating an online search strategy.

67. List three search commands and explain how each command enhances online results.

68. Describe three ways in which a student can critically evaluate Internet sources.

ANSWER KEY FOR CHAPTER 11

1. False (p. 62)	24. True (p. 66)	47. A (p. 61)
2. False (p. 63)	25. False (p. 66)	48. meta-search (p. 63)
3. True (p. 63)	26. True (p. 66)	49. relevance (p. 63)
4. False (p. 63)	27. True (p. 61)	50. subject or human (p. 64)
5. True (pp. 63–64)	28. True (p. 61)	51. password (p. 65)
6. False (p. 63)	29. False (p. 61)	52. virtual (p. 65)
7. True (p. 62)	30. True (p. 61)	53. invisible (p. 65)
8. False (p. 64)	31. D (p. 60)	54. subject or human (p. 64)
9. True (p. 64)	32. C (p. 62)	55. Boolean operators (p. 66)
10. True (p. 64)	33. D (p. 63)	56. NOT (p. 66)
11. True (p. 62)	34. A (p. 64)	57. domain (p. 61)
12. False (p. 64)	35. D (p. 62)	58. tilde (p. 61)
13. True (p. 64)	36. B (p. 62)	59. human or subject (p. 64)
14. True (pp. 64–65)	37. D (p. 64)	60. (No answer, pp. 61–62)
15. False (p. 65)	38. B (pp. 63–64)	61. (No answer, pp. 62–63)
16. True (p. 65)	39. B (p. 64)	62. (No answer, p. 64)
17. True (p. 65)	40. B (p. 63)	63. (No answer, p. 64)
18. False (p. 65)	41. D (p. 65)	64. (No answer, p. 64)
19. True (p. 62)	42. B (p. 64)	65. (No answer, p. 65)
20. False (pp. 61–62)	43. C (p. 64)	66. (No answer, p. 66)
21. True (pp 61–62)	44. B (p. 66)	67. (No answer, p. 66)
22. True (p. 64)	45. B (p. 66)	68. (No answer, p. 61)
23. True (p. 66)	46. D (p. 66)	

12 Organizing Main and Supporting Points

TRUE/FALSE QUESTIONS

1. The structure of a speech is composed of three main parts: an introduction, a body, and a conclusion.

2. The body of a speech establishes the speech purpose and shows its relevance to the audience.

3. The introduction of a speech tells listeners where they are going.

4. Main points express the key ideas and major themes of the speech.

5. The first step in creating main points is to identify the central ideas and themes of the speech.

6. The thesis statement expresses the goal of the speech, whereas the specific purpose expresses the theme or central idea of the speech.

7. Research shows that audiences can comfortably take in between eight and ten main points.

8. Listeners have better recall of the main points made at the beginning and at the end of a speech than of those made in between.

9. To help the audience remember what you say, use as few main points as possible.

10. A main point should not introduce more than two ideas.

11. Whenever possible, main points should be stated in parallel form.

12. Each main point should be expressed as an interrogative sentence.

13. Presenting each main point as a declarative statement emphasizes the point and makes it stand out from the others.

14. Supporting points represent the supporting material or evidence that a speaker has gathered to justify the main points.

15. In an outline, supporting points appear in a superordinate position to the main points.

16. The most common outline format is the Roman numeral outline.

17. In a Roman numeral outline, third-level points are enumerated with Arabic numerals.

18. In an outline, indentation indicates different levels of points.

19. Indentations in an outline are used to arrange supporting points.

20. A well-organized speech is characterized by unity, coherence, and balance.

21. *Coherence* refers to a speech containing only those points that are implied by the purpose and thesis statements.

22. In speeches that have unity, each point focuses on a single idea.

23. *Unity* refers to clarity and logical consistency.

24. The speech body should follow logically from the introduction, and the conclusion should follow logically from the body.

25. Ideas that are coordinate are given equal weight.

26. In an outline, subordinate points are indicated by their parallel alignment, and coordinate points are indicated by their indentation below the more important points.

27. In an outline, Main Point II is subordinate to Main Point I, and Subpoint A is coordinate to Main Point I.

28. The principle of balance suggests that appropriate emphasis or weight be given to each part of the speech relative to the other parts and to the theme.

29. The introduction of a speech should always be the longest part.

30. Assigning each main point at least two supporting points is one aspect of balance.

31. Words, phrases, or sentences that tie the speech ideas together and enable the speaker to move smoothly from one point to the next are called *transitions*.

32. Transitions may be stated as rhetorical questions, but they should not be stated in restate-forecast form.

MULTIPLE-CHOICE QUESTIONS

33. The speech conclusion brings closure to the speech by
    A) restating the purpose.
    B) reiterating why the purpose is relevant to the audience.
    C) leaving audience members with something to think about.
    D) doing all of the above.

34. The body of a speech consists of
    A) thesis statements and introductions.
    B) main points, supporting points, and transitions.
    C) specific purpose statements and internal summaries.
    D) all of the above.

35. Which of the following expresses the speech goal?
    A) specific speech purpose   C) main points
    B) thesis statement   D) all of the above

36. Which of the following helps to determine the number of main points for a speech?
    A) the topic
    B) the amount of material to be covered
    C) the length of the speech
    D) all of the above

37. Research indicates that audiences prefer speeches that contain _____ main points.
    A) one to two   C) five to ten
    B) two to seven   D) at least six

38. Facts, statistics, testimonies, and narratives are all examples of
    A) main points.   C) supporting material.
    B) transitions.   D) none of the above.

39. A well-organized speech is characterized by
    A) unity, coherence, and balance.
    B) unity, coordination, and balance.
    C) unity, subordination, and coherence.
    D) unity, coordination, and subordination.

40. Effective transitions move listeners from
    A) one main point to the next.
    B) a main point to a supporting point.
    C) one supporting point to another supporting point.
    D) all of the above.

FILL-IN-THE-BLANK QUESTIONS

41. The _____ of a speech establishes the speech purpose and shows its relevance to the audience.

42. _____ points express the key ideas and major themes of the speech.

43. The _____ expresses the goal of the speech.

44. The _____ expresses the theme or central idea of the speech.

45. A main point should not introduce more than _____ idea(s).

46. _____ points represent the supporting material or evidence that a speaker has gathered.

47. _____ is the most common outline format.

48. A well-organized speech is characterized by unity, _____ , and balance.

49. A speech exhibits _____ when it contains only those points that are implied by the purpose and thesis statements.

50. Ideas that are _____ are given equal weight.

51. Points in an outline that are indicated by their parallel alignment are known as _____ points.

52. Points in an outline that are indicated by their indentation below the more important points are known as _____ points.

53. The principle of _____ suggests that appropriate emphasis or weight be given to each part of the speech relative to the other parts and to the theme.

54. The _____ of a speech should always be the longest part.

55. Assigning each main point at least two supporting points is one aspect of _____ .

56. Words, phrases, or sentences that tie the speech ideas together and enable the speaker to move smoothly from one point to the next are called _____ .

ESSAY AND SHORT ANSWER QUESTIONS

57. Explain how the specific purpose and thesis statements serve as guideposts in creating main points.

58. Why should a speaker adhere to using only two to seven main points?

59. Discuss why the body of the speech should be the longest part.

60. Why is it important to make the speech introduction and conclusion roughly the same length?

61. Define *unity, coherence,* and *balance,* and give an example of each.

ANSWER KEY FOR CHAPTER 12

1. True (p. 69)
2. False (p. 69)
3. True (p. 69)
4. True (p. 69)
5. True (p. 69)
6. False (p. 69)
7. False (p. 70)
8. True (p. 70)
9. True (p. 70)
10. False (p. 70)
11. True (p. 70)
12. False (p. 70)
13. True (p. 70)
14. True (p. 70)
15. False (p. 71)
16. True (p. 71)
17. True (p. 71)
18. True (p. 71)
19. True (p. 71)
20. True (p. 72)
21. False (p. 72)

22. True (p. 72)
23. False (p. 72)
24. True (p. 72)
25. True (p. 72)
26. False (p. 72)
27. False (p. 72)
28. True (p. 73)
29. False (p. 73)
30. True (p. 73)
31. True (p. 73)
32. False (p. 74)
33. D (p. 69)
34. B (p. 69)
35. A (p. 69)
36. D (p. 70)
37. B (p. 70)
38. C (p. 70)
39. A (p. 72)
40. D (p. 73)
41. introduction (p. 69)
42. Main (p. 69)

43. specific purpose statement (p. 69)
44. thesis statement (p. 69)
45. one (p. 69)
46. Supporting (p. 70)
47. Roman numeral outline (p. 71)
48. coherence (p. 72)
49. unity (p. 72)
50. coordinate (p. 72)
51. coordinate (p. 72)
52. subordinate (p. 72)
53. balance (p. 73)
54. body (p. 73)
55. balance (p. 73)
56. transitions (p. 73)
57. (No answer, p. 69)
58. (No answer, p. 70)
59. (No answer, p. 73)
60. (No answer, p. 73)
61. (No answer, pp. 72–73)

13 *Selecting an Organizational Pattern*

TRUE/FALSE QUESTIONS

1. Some common organizational arrangements for public speeches are topical, chronological, spatial, causal, problem-solution, narrative, and circle.

2. A topical pattern of arrangement is most appropriate when each main point is of relatively equal importance.

3. In a topical pattern, points can be arranged in any order without negatively affecting each other or the speech purpose.

4. Chronological arrangements give the speaker the greatest freedom to structure main points according to the audience's interests and the circumstances of the occasion.

5. A chronological pattern of arrangement follows the natural sequential order of the main points.

6. A speech describing a series of events in the development of a new idea calls for a spatial pattern of arrangement.

7. Topics that involve time lines or a series of sequential steps require the chronological pattern of arrangement.

8. The spatial pattern describes the physical arrangement of a place, scene, or object.

9. The causal pattern relates a cause to its effects.

10. It is never appropriate to present the effect first and the causes subsequently in the causal pattern.

11. Speakers usually select a causal arrangement when the general speech purpose is to persuade.

12. The problem-solution pattern of arrangement may have more than two main points.

13. The function of the problem-solution pattern is to demonstrate the nature and significance of a problem and to provide justification for a proposed solution.

14. The chronological pattern of arrangement assumes a largely Asian orientation to time.

MULTIPLE-CHOICE QUESTIONS

15. To stress natural divisions in a topic, a speaker should use which pattern of arrangement?
    A) topical
    B) chronological
    C) spatial
    D) causal

16. To describe a series of developments in time or a set of actions that occur sequentially, a speaker should use which pattern of arrangement?
    A) topical
    B) chronological
    C) spatial
    D) causal

17. To explain the physical arrangement of a place, a scene, or an object, a speaker should use which pattern of arrangement?
    A) topical
    B) chronological
    C) spatial
    D) causal

18. To discuss a topic in terms of its underlying causes, a speaker should use which pattern of arrangement?
    A) topical
    B) chronological
    C) causal
    D) circle

19. To demonstrate the nature and significance of a problem and provide justification for a proposed solution, a speaker should use which pattern of arrangement?
    A) topical
    B) chronological
    C) causal
    D) problem-solution

FILL-IN-THE-BLANK QUESTIONS

20. A(n) _____ pattern of arrangement is most appropriate when each main point is of relatively equal importance.

21. In a(n) _____ pattern, points can be arranged in any order without negatively affecting each other or the speech purpose.

22. The _____ pattern of arrangement gives the speaker the greatest freedom to structure main points according to the audience's interests and the circumstances of the occasion.

23. A(n) _____ pattern of arrangement follows the natural sequential order of the main points.

24. A speech describing a series of events in the development of a new idea calls for a _____ pattern of arrangement.

25. Topics that involve time lines or a series of sequential steps require the _____ pattern of arrangement.

26. The _____ pattern describes the physical arrangement of a place, scene, or object.

27. The _____ pattern relates a cause to its effects.

28. The function of the _____ pattern is to demonstrate the nature and significance of a problem and to provide justification for a proposed solution.

29. The _____ pattern involves conveying ideas through the medium of a story.

ESSAY AND SHORT ANSWER QUESTIONS

30. When is the chronological pattern of arrangement appropriate for a speech?

31. Give an example of the spatial pattern of arrangement.

32. Explain the difference between the causal and the problem-solution patterns of arrangement.

33. Explain and provide an example of how a speech can use more than one organizational pattern.

ANSWER KEY FOR CHAPTER 13

1. True (p. 76)	12. True (p. 79)	23. chronological (p. 77)
2. True (p. 81)	13. True (p. 79)	24. chronological (p. 77)
3. True (p. 81)	14. False (p. 77)	25. chronological (p. 77)
4. False (p. 77)	15. A (p. 81)	26. spatial (p. 77)
5. True (p. 77)	16. B (p. 77)	27. causal (p. 78)
6. False (p. 77)	17. C (p. 77)	28. problem-solution (p. 79)
7. True (p. 77)	18. C (p. 78)	29. narrative (pp. 81–82)
8. True (p. 77)	19. D (p. 79)	30. (No answer, p. 77)
9. True (p. 78)	20. topical (p. 81)	31. (No answer, p. 77)
10. False (p. 79)	21. topical (p. 81)	32. (No answer, pp. 78–79)
11. False (p. 78)	22. topical (p. 81)	33. (No answer)

14 *Using Outline Formats*

1. When developing a speech, a speaker should create two separate outlines: a working outline and a delivery outline.

2. Studies show that speech organization does not affect audience perceptions of speaker credibility.

3. Outlines are critical to organizing a speech.

4. When a speech is very disorganized, audiences react negatively.

5. The purpose of a speaking outline is to refine and finalize the specific purpose statement, firm up and organize main points, and develop supporting points to substantiate them.

6. Working outlines are meant to be changed as a speaker works through the information and ideas collected for a speech.

7. Once the speaking outline is complete, the speaker should transfer its ideas to the working outline.

8. Speeches may be outlined in complete sentences, phrases, or key words.

9. Sentence outlines represent the full text of the speech.

10. Generally, sentence outlines are used for speaking outlines.

11. A sentence outline is effective for an inexperienced speaker.

12. A phrase outline is effective when the material is highly technical and exact sentence structure is critical.

13. The first step in outlining a speech is to select your topic.

14. Speaking professionals recommend that the actual speaking outline be prepared using a full-sentence format.

15. Writing an outline in full sentences builds speaker confidence.

16. In the working outline, each section of the speech (introduction, body, and conclusion) should be labeled.

17. A phrase outline is the briefest form of outline.

18. A phrase outline uses a partial construction of the sentence form of each point.

19. Phrase outlines or key-word outlines are recommended over sentence outlines in the delivery of most speeches.

20. Phrase outlines are the preferred format for speaking outlines.

21. The speaking outline should be prepared on full sheets of paper.

22. In the speaking outline, the introduction and the conclusion are among the main points.

23. The speech introduction and conclusion should be placed on separate notecards.

24. A speaking outline should contain brief parenthetical notes indicating transitions, sources to cite, and presentation aids.

MULTIPLE-CHOICE QUESTIONS

25. Which of the following outlines is an in-process document to be revised and rearranged until the speaker is satisfied with it?
    A) working
    B) speaking
    C) sentence
    D) key-word

26. Which of the following outlines should be prepared in a full-sentence format?
    A) working
    B) speaking
    C) phrase
    D) key-word

27. Which of the following outlines uses a partial construction of the sentence form of each point?
    A) working
    B) speaking
    C) sentence
    D) phrase

28. Which of the following outlines uses a few words associated with each specific point?
    A) working
    B) speaking
    C) key-word
    D) phrase

29. Which of the following outlines offers the most protection against memory lapses?
    A) working
    B) speaking
    C) key-word
    D) sentence

30. Which type of outline is easiest to handle and follow if the speaker is well rehearsed?
    A) working
    B) speaking
    C) key-word
    D) none of the above

31. The speaking outline should
    A) be written on small notecards.
    B) be written in large print.
    C) include transitions.
    D) do all of the above.

FILL-IN-THE-BLANK QUESTIONS

32. When developing a speech, the speaker should create two separate outlines: a _____ outline and a _____ outline.

33. The purpose of the _____ outline is to refine and finalize the specific purpose statement, firm up and organize main points, and develop supporting points to substantiate them.

34. A type of outline that is meant to be changed as the speaker works through the information and ideas for a speech is called a(n) _____ outline.

35. Once the working outline is complete, the speaker should transfer its ideas to the _____ outline.

36. Speeches may be outlined in complete sentences, with key words, or in _____ .

37. A type of outline that represents the full text of the speech is known as a _____ outline.

38. Generally, _____ outlines are preferred for speaking outlines.

39. A(n) _____ outline is effective for an inexperienced speaker.

40. A(n) _____ outline is effective when the material is highly technical and exact sentence structure is critical.

41. A _____ outline permits more eye contact, greater freedom of movement, and better control of your thoughts and actions.

42. In the _____ outline, each section of the speech (introduction, body, and conclusion) should be labeled.

43. A(n) _____ outline is the briefest form of outline.

44. A(n) _____ outline uses partial construction of the sentence form of each point.

45. A type of outline not recommended in the delivery of most speeches is the _____ outline.

46. _____ outlines are the preferred format for speaking outlines.

47. A(n) _____ outline should contain brief parenthetical notes indicating transitions, sources to cite, and presentation aids.

ESSAY AND SHORT ANSWER QUESTIONS

48. How can a speaker prepare a speech using a working outline?

49. Why should a working outline be prepared in a full-sentence format?

50. Identify the steps involved in creating a working outline.

51. Explain the difference between a phrase outline and a key-word outline.

52. List one advantage and one disadvantage of a sentence outline.

53. In a speaking outline, how should a speaker indicate transitions, sources to cite, and presentation aids to be used in the speech?

54. Identify the steps involved in creating a speaking outline.

ANSWER KEY FOR CHAPTER 14

1. True (p. 83)
2. False (p. 83)
3. True (p. 83)
4. True (p. 83)
5. False (p. 85)
6. True (p. 83)
7. False (p. 85)
8. True (p. 84)
9. True (p. 84)
10. False (p. 85)
11. True (p. 85)
12. False (p. 85)
13. True (p. 85)
14. False (p. 84)
15. True (p. 84)
16. True (p. 84)
17. False (p. 85)
18. True (p. 85)

19. True (pp. 85–86)
20. False (p. 85)
21. False (p. 87)
22. False (p. 85)
23. True (p. 86)
24. True (p. 86)
25. A (p. 83)
26. A (p. 83)
27. D (p. 85)
28. C (p. 86)
29. D (p. 84)
30. C (p. 86)
31. D (pp. 85–86)
32. working; speaking or delivery (pp. 83, 85)
33. working (p. 83)
34. working (p. 83)
35. speaking or delivery (p. 85)
36. phrases (p. 85)
37. sentence (p. 84)

38. key-word (p. 86)
39. sentence (p. 84)
40. sentence (p. 84)
41. key-word (p. 86)
42. working (p. 85)
43. key-word (p. 86)
44. phrase (p. 85)
45. sentence (p. 84)
46. Key-word (p. 86)
47. speaking (p. 85)
48. (No answer, p. 83)
49. (No answer, p. 84)
50. (No answer, p. 83)
51. (No answer, pp. 85–86)
52. (No answer, p. 84)
53. (No answer, p. 86)
54. (No answer, p. 85)

Developing the Introduction *15*
and Conclusion

TRUE/FALSE QUESTIONS

1. If the body of the speech is well-developed, it is sometimes an effective technique to deliver the introduction and conclusion spontaneously, without preparation.

2. The introduction and the conclusion of the speech are more important than the body.

3. A compelling introduction and a memorable conclusion can ultimately make the difference between a great speech and one that is merely satisfactory.

4. The choices a speaker makes about the introduction of a speech do not affect the outcome of the entire speech.

5. Audience members decide in the first five seconds of a speech whether they will give their full attention to the speaker and believe what he or she has to say.

6. Supporting material should not be used to open a speech.

7. The first challenge a speaker faces in developing an introduction is to win the audience's attention.

8. In an introduction, using a quotation from someone who is not famous will discredit the speaker.

9. Using a story in an introduction can make the speaker's ideas concrete and colorful.

10. After using a real or hypothetical story to introduce a speech, the speaker should be sure to explain exactly what the story means.

11. A rhetorical question posed by the speaker seeks a direct response from the audience.

12. Polling audience members during the speech introduction is an effective way to gain their attention.

13. Posing questions draws the audience's attention to what you are about to say.

14. Speakers who introduce their speeches with startling statements or unusual information are ineffective in gaining the audience's attention.

15. Introducing a speech with a short joke or a funny story sets a positive tone for what is to follow.

16. When using humor in an introduction, the speaker should keep in mind that the humor should relate to the speech topic and occasion.

17. Introductions that include references to the speech occasion and the audience tend to capture audience attention and establish goodwill.

18. Focusing on the audience in the introduction demonstrates interest and respect.

19. Focusing on facts rather than on the audience in the introduction builds speaker credibility.

20. The speech introduction should capture the audience's attention, but it does not need to delve into the topic and purpose of the speech.

21. When speakers use the technique of previewing in an introduction, they state the main points of the speech.

22. Introductory previews should be long and complicated.

23. Previewing helps the audience mentally organize a speech.

24. A speech introduction should identify the speech topic and purpose.

25. Audience members are usually motivated to listen to a message they think is relevant to them.

26. Explaining to audience members what they have to gain by listening to you is not effective in motivating an audience to accept the goals of your speech.

27. To build credibility in the introduction, a speaker should make a simple statement of his or her qualifications for speaking on the topic.

28. The introduction should be prepared first, as it is the first part of the speech.

29. As a rule, the length of the introduction should be no more than 20 to 25 percent of the speech body.

30. A conclusion signals the end of the speech and provides closure.

31. A transition statement or phrase is one way to alert the audience that a speech is coming to an end.

32. Audiences appreciate it when speakers say "in conclusion" and then keep speaking for a long period of time.

33. A speaker can effectively signal closure by manner of delivery.

34. A conclusion gives the speaker the opportunity to drive home his or her purpose and a final chance to reinforce the main points of the speech.

35. In the conclusion, the speaker should not reiterate the topic and speech purpose.

36. A strong conclusion challenges audience members to put to use what the speaker has taught them.

37. In informative speeches, the concluding challenge comes in the form of a call to action.

38. Quotations, stories, and questions are appropriate ways to conclude a speech.

39. Using a quotation that captures the essence of the speech can be a very effective way to close a speech.

40. Rhetorical questions are not effective conclusions.

MULTIPLE-CHOICE QUESTIONS

41. A speech introduction is designed to
    A) arouse the audience's attention and motivate the audience to accept the speaker's goals.
    B) provide an in-depth discussion of the topic.
    C) review and discuss all the main points of a speech.
    D) do all of the above.

42. Which of the following can be used to effectively introduce or conclude a speech?
    A) examples   C) facts and statistics
    B) stories   D) all of the above

43. The first challenge faced by the speaker in the introduction of the speech is to win the audience's
    A) attention.   C) admiration.
    B) approval.   D) acceptance.

44. In her speech about friendship, Becky opened by stating, "As Vanessa Smith has written, 'Many people will walk in and out of your life, but only true friends will leave footprints in your heart.'" Becky began her introduction by using
    A) repetition.   C) a quotation.
    B) a startling statement.   D) imagery.

45. Using a story as a speech introduction
    A) personalizes issues.
    B) makes ideas irrelevant.
    C) discourages identification.
    D) does none of the above.

46. Speakers frequently base their startling statements on
    A) statistics.
    B) humor.
    C) attitudes.
    D) all of the above.

47. Speech humor should always match
    A) the audience.
    B) the topic.
    C) the occasion.
    D) all of the above.

48. An effective introduction should
    A) capture your audience's attention.
    B) comprise at least 25 percent of your total speech.
    C) be prepared before the body of the speech.
    D) be all of the above.

49. Previewing the speech in the introduction
    A) tells the audience the order in which the main points will be addressed.
    B) addresses the tone rather than the organization of the speech.
    C) often "gives away" the entire content of the speech.
    D) does all of the above.

50. A good introduction demonstrates why the audience should care above all about a speaker's
    A) opinions.
    B) topic.
    C) purpose.
    D) supporting material.

51. During the speech introduction, the audience decides whether they are interested in the topic and the speaker. To build credibility, a speaker should establish his or her
    A) family background.
    B) supporting material.
    C) qualifications.
    D) logos.

52. Generally, the introduction should be brief and no more than _____ percent of the speech body.
    A) 5 to 10
    B) 10 to 15
    C) 15 to 20
    D) 20 to 25

53. Conclusions provide
    A) the speaker with the opportunity to drive home the speech purpose.
    B) the speaker with a final chance to make an impression that accomplishes the speech goals.
    C) the audience with a sense of logical and emotional closure.
    D) all of the above.

54. An effective conclusion should always
    A) quote poetry.
    B) make the speech memorable.
    C) introduce the last main point.
    D) do all of the above.

55. The conclusion should be about _____ the length of the speech.
    A) one-half
    B) one-third
    C) one-sixth
    D) one-eighth

56. Speech conclusions fulfill which of the following functions?
    A) alert the audience that the speech is coming to an end
    B) summarize the key points of the speech
    C) challenge the audience to respond
    D) all of the above

57. The summary portion of the speech conclusion should *not*
    A) "tell the audience what you've told them."
    B) mention each main point of the speech.
    C) mention each supporting point of the speech.
    D) comment on the significance of each main point.

58. A concluding challenge by a speaker that asks an audience to act in response to the speech is termed a
    A) persuasive attempt.
    B) call to action.
    C) reiteration.
    D) signpost.

59. Listeners are most likely to remember and act on a speech that
    A) uses many statistics.
    B) ends with a strong conclusion.
    C) begins with a quotation.
    D) does all of the above.

ESSAY AND SHORT ANSWER QUESTIONS

60. Explain how the speech introduction prepares an audience to listen to a speech.

61. Why is it important for a speaker to prepare the introduction and conclusion just as thoroughly as he or she prepares the speech body?

62. List three types of supporting material that are effective in opening a speech.

63. Give an example of a quotation to introduce a speech.

64. Write a brief introduction that begins with the following quotation by Maya Angelou: "When people show you who they are, believe them."

65. Give an example of a rhetorical question to introduce a speech.

66. Name two general guidelines for using a story in a speech.

67. During the introduction, how can a speaker express a genuine interest in the audience?

68. Give an example of previewing in an introduction.

69. Why is it so important for a speaker to use the introduction to establish the relevance of the topic to the audience?

70. Explain why the introduction should be written after the speech body.

71. List three functions of a conclusion.

72. How can a conclusion effectively summarize the main points and goals of a speech?

73. Explain how a challenge issued during a conclusion varies for an informative and a persuasive speech.

74. Discuss three ways a speaker can make a conclusion memorable.

75. Give an example of a concluding rhetorical question.

76. Name three guidelines for preparing a conclusion.

ANSWER KEY FOR CHAPTER 15

1. False (p. 89)	27. True (p. 93)	53. D (pp. 93–94)
2. False (p. 89)	28. False (p. 89)	54. B (p. 94)
3. True (p. 89)	29. False (p. 89)	55. C (p. 94)
4. False (p. 89)	30. True (p. 94)	56. D (p. 94)
5. False (p. 89)	31. True (p. 94)	57. C (p. 94)
6. False (p. 90)	32. False (p. 94)	58. B (p. 95)
7. True (p. 90)	33. True (p. 94)	59. B (p. 96)
8. False (p. 90)	34. True (p. 94)	60. (No answer, p. 89)
9. True (p. 90)	35. False (p. 95)	61. (No answer, p. 89)
10. False (p. 90)	36. True (p. 95)	62. (No answer, p. 90)
11. False (p. 90)	37. False (p. 95)	63. (No answer, p. 90)
12. True (p. 90)	38. True (p. 96)	64. (No answer)
13. True (p. 90)	39. True (p. 96)	65. (No answer, p. 90)
14. False (p. 90)	40. False (p. 96)	66. (No answer, p. 90)
15. True (p. 90)	41. A (pp. 89–90)	67. (No answer, p. 91)
16. True (p. 90)	42. D (p. 90)	68. (No answer, p. 91)
17. True (p. 91)	43. A (p. 90)	69. (No answer, p. 92)
18. True (p. 91)	44. C (p. 90)	70. (No answer, p. 89)
19. False (pp. 92–93)	45. A (p. 90)	71. (No answer, p. 94)
20. False (p. 91)	46. A (p. 90)	72. (No answer, p. 94)
21. True (p. 91)	47. D (p. 90)	73. (No answer, p. 95)
22. False (p. 91)	48. A (p. 89)	74. (No answer, p. 96)
23. True (p. 91)	49. A (p. 91)	75. (No answer, p. 96)
24. True (p. 91)	50. B (p. 91)	76. (No answer, p. 94)
25. True (p. 92)	51. C (p. 93)	
26. False (p. 92)	52. B (p. 89)	

16 *Using Language*

1. Rhetorical devices are techniques of language that speakers use to express their ideas in order to achieve their speech purpose.

2. Since few contemporary audiences are culturally diverse, a speaker need not be aware of or sensitive to cultural variations in language.

3. Cultural sensitivity is a purely unconscious, instinctive way of judging cultural beliefs, norms, or traditions that are different from your own.

4. Language that relies on unfounded assumptions, negative descriptions, or stereotypes of a given group's characteristics is termed *biased language.*

5. The specialized language of a given profession is called *filibustering.*

6. Listeners prefer complex language over simple language in a speech.

7. Abstract language is specific, tangible, and definite.

8. The words *old, thing, big,* and *bad* are examples of abstract language.

9. A speaker who describes activities and objects with colorful and concrete language helps create a vivid image for the audience or appeals to their senses.

10. A metaphor compares one thing to another, using *like* or *as* to do so.

11. An analogy compares an unfamiliar concept to a more familiar one in order to increase audience understanding of the unfamiliar concept.

12. *Love is a rose* is an example of a simile.

13. A speaker's use or misuse of language has a significant effect on the level of credibility he or she establishes with the audience.

14. Figures of speech include similes, metaphors, and analogies.

15. The connotative meaning is the literal, or dictionary, definition of a word.

16. In the sentence *Tom invited Maria on a date,* the active voice is used.

17. Repetition is an effective strategy for using language in a speech.

18. Alliteration is the arrangement of words, phrases, or sentences in a similar form.

19. Parallelism is the repetition of the same sounds, usually initial consonants, in two or more neighboring words or syllables.

MULTIPLE-CHOICE QUESTIONS

20. The term *biased language* refers to language that is
    A) ageist or homophobic.
    B) sexist or racist.
    C) both A and B.
    D) neither A nor B.

21. A speaker who uses vivid imagery
    A) diminishes meaning.
    B) distracts listeners from the main point of the speech.
    C) invites listeners to use their imaginations.
    D) does none of the above.

22. In Leeza's presentation on her graduate school experiences, she said, "Graduate school is an uphill battle." Leeza used which figure of speech?
    A) simile   C) analogy
    B) metaphor   D) alliteration

23. Forms of expression that create striking comparisons to help listeners visualize, identify with, and understand the speaker's ideas are called
    A) alliteration.   C) figures of speech.
    B) libelous language.   D) conjunctions.

24. *His character plays a rocking, rolling, roaring, raging role.* This statement best illustrates which of the following techniques?
    A) simile   C) personification
    B) metaphor   D) alliteration

25. *His lies are a house of cards.* This statement best illustrates which of the following techniques?
    A) simile   C) personification
    B) metaphor   D) alliteration

26. Effective speakers are careful to use language that is appropriate to
    A) the audience.   C) the subject matter.
    B) the occasion.   D) all of the above.

27. The literal, dictionary definition of a word is its
    A) hyperbolic meaning.   C) denotative meaning.
    B) analagous meaning.   D) connotative meaning.

28. When people disagree about the meaning of a word, they are responding to the word's
    A) denotative meaning.   C) libelous meaning.
    B) connotative meaning.   D) abstract meaning.

29. One way that a speaker can leave a lasting impression on listeners is to incorporate oral language that is artfully arranged and infused with rhythm. One device that helps a speaker accomplish this specific purpose is
    A) repetition.   C) analogy.
    B) personification.   D) none of the above.

30. Parallelism can be used by a speaker
    A) to create a powerful and poetic effect for the audience.
    B) to orally enumerate the speech's main points.
    C) in the form of pairs or triads.
    D) in all of the above ways.

FILL-IN-THE-BLANK QUESTIONS

31. Cultural _____ is a conscious attempt to be considerate of cultural beliefs, norms, or traditions different from your own.

32. Language that relies on unfounded assumptions, negative descriptions, or stereotypes of a given group's characteristics is termed _____ language.

33. The specialized language of a given profession is called _____ .

34. _____ language is specific, tangible, and definite.

35. A(n) _____ explicitly compares one thing to another, using *like* or *as* to do so.

36. A(n) _____ compares an unfamiliar concept to a more familiar one in order to increase audience understanding of the unfamiliar concept.

37. The _____ meaning of a word is its literal, or dictionary, definition.

38. The _____ meaning of a word is the special association that different people bring to bear on it.

39. _____ is the repetition of the same sounds, usually initial consonants, in two or more neighboring words or syllables.

ESSAY AND SHORT ANSWER QUESTIONS

40. Why does a speaker's use of jargon often exasperate an audience?

41. Explain why speakers should strive for simplicity in language.

42. How can a speaker create vivid imagery for the audience?

43. Explain the difference between a metaphor and a simile.

44. Explain and give an example of a rhetorical device that a speaker can use to create effective rhythm and a lasting impression in his or her speech.

ANSWER KEY FOR CHAPTER 16

1. True (p. 97)
2. False (p. 97)
3. False (p. 97)
4. True (p. 97)
5. False (p. 98)
6. False (p. 98)
7. False (p. 98)
8. True (pp. 98–99)
9. True (p. 99)
10. False (p. 99)
11. True (p. 99)
12. False (p. 99)
13. True (p. 99)
14. True (p. 99)
15. False (p. 100)

16. True (p. 100)
17. True (p. 101)
18. False (p. 101)
19. False (p. 102)
20. C (p. 97)
21. C (p. 99)
22. B (p. 99)
23. C (p. 99)
24. D (p. 101)
25. B (p. 99)
26. D (p. 99)
27. C (p. 100)
28. B (p. 100)
29. A (p. 101)
30. D (p. 102)

31. sensitivity (p. 97)
32. biased (p. 97)
33. jargon (p. 98)
34. Concrete (pp. 98–99)
35. simile (p. 99)
36. analogy (p. 99)
37. denotative (p. 100)
38. connotative (p. 100)
39. Alliteration (p. 101)
40. (No answer, p. 98)
41. (No answer, p. 98)
42. (No answer, p. 99)
43. (No answer, p. 99)
44. (No answer, p. 101)

TRUE/FALSE QUESTIONS

1. It is important for a speaker to incorporate elements of conversational style in delivering a speech.

2. Effective delivery is quite different from everyday conversation in that it relies on stylized gestures.

3. Delivery is a critical part of successful speechmaking.

4. Speakers who lack enthusiasm often lose their audience's attention.

5. A speaker can build rapport with his or her audience by making the message relevant to the audience and by using direct delivery.

6. Speaking from a manuscript is most useful when the speaker is required to be very precise in his or her message.

7. Speaking from memory is the most natural way to deliver a message.

8. Speaking from a manuscript is considered best for brief speeches, such as toasts and introductions.

9. Delivering a speech without prior preparation is called *speaking extemporaneously*.

10. Most public speeches are delivered extemporaneously.

11. Impromptu delivery is the most widely used form of delivery in public speaking.

MULTIPLE-CHOICE QUESTIONS

12. Effective speech delivery should be all of the following:
    A) natural, monotone, confident, and comfortable.
    B) natural, self-deprecating, direct, and abstract.
    C) natural, enthusiastic, confident, and direct.
    D) natural, confident, extremely formal, and animated.

13. A speaker can feel confident that his or her delivery has a relaxed, natural quality if
    A) the message is presented with cheerfulness.
    B) the speaker's behavior does not call undue attention to itself.
    C) the speaker focuses more on self and less on audience.
    D) all of the above are accomplished.

14. A speaker can establish a direct connection with listeners by
    A) maintaining eye contact.
    B) using animated facial expressions.
    C) using a friendly tone of voice.
    D) doing all of the above.

15. Speaking from a manuscript
    A) is useful when precise messages are required.
    B) encourages eye contact.
    C) encourages naturalness.
    D) is best in informal settings.

16. In terms of preparation, the most time-consuming method of speech delivery is
    A) extemporaneous speaking.
    B) speaking from memory.
    C) impromptu speaking.
    D) speaking from manuscript.

17. The formal name for speaking from memory is
    A) oratory.   C) impromptu.
    B) manuscript.   D) extemporaneous.

18. Which type of delivery worries speakers because they have little time to gather their thoughts and composure?
    A) memorized   C) impromptu
    B) manuscript   D) extemporaneous

19. The word *impromptu* means
    A) improvised and unpracticed. C) lively and personal.
    B) provocative and spontaneous. D) none of the above.

20. Which type of delivery falls somewhere between impromptu and memorized?
    A) unpracticed   C) extemporaneous
    B) manuscript   D) all of the above

21. The method of speech delivery that is most flexible for the speaker and preferred by listeners is
    A) extemporaneous speaking.   C) impromptu speaking.
    B) speaking from memory.   D) speaking from manuscript.

FILL-IN-THE-BLANK QUESTIONS

22. In a speech, the skillful application of natural conversational behavior is termed effective _____ .

23. Effective delivery has many elements in common with everyday _____ .

24. Speaking from _____ is most useful when the speaker is required to be very precise in his or her message.

25. The delivery method known as _____ speaking is the most natural way to deliver a speech.

26. Speaking from _____ requires that the speaker recall exact words, which runs the risk of the speaker having a mental block at some point.

27. When a speaker delivers a speech without any prior preparation, he or she is giving a(n) _____ delivery.

28. Speaking from _____ is an appropriate type of delivery for brief speeches, such as toasts and introductions.

29. Most public speeches are given using _____ delivery.

30. Speaking _____ is the term for giving a prepared and practiced speech without memorizing it or reading it word for word from a text.

ESSAY AND SHORT ANSWER QUESTIONS

31. Explain why speech delivery should strive for natural, rather than theatrical, behavior.

32. How can a speaker project a sense of confidence and competence?

33. List three ways for a speaker to establish a direct connection with an audience when delivering a speech.

34. Identify two ways in which speakers can make a delivery seem more natural when they are reading from a prepared text.

35. Why should a speaker avoid memorizing an entire speech?

36. List two tips for impromptu speaking.

37. Compare and contrast these two methods of speech delivery: speaking impromptu and speaking extemporaneously.

38. As an audience member, which of the four methods of speech delivery do you prefer? Give three reasons why you prefer this particular method.

ANSWER KEY FOR CHAPTER 17

1. True (p. 104)
2. False (p. 104)
3. True (p. 104)
4. True (p. 104)
5. True (p. 104)
6. True (p. 105)
7. False (p. 105)
8. False (p. 105)
9. False (p. 107)
10. True (p. 107)
11. False (p. 106)
12. C (p. 104)
13. B (p. 104)

14. D (p. 104)
15. A (p. 105)
16. B (p. 105)
17. A (p. 105)
18. C (p. 106)
19. A (p. 106)
20. C (p. 107)
21. A (p. 107)
22. delivery (p. 104)
23. conversation (p. 104)
24. manuscript (p. 105)
25. extemporaneous (p. 107)
26. memory (p. 105)

27. impromptu (p. 106)
28. memory (p. 105)
29. extemporaneous (p. 107)
30. extemporaneously (p. 107)
31. (No answer, p. 104)
32. (No answer, p. 104)
33. (No answer, p. 104)
34. (No answer, p. 105)
35. (No answer, p. 105)
36. (No answer, p. 106)
37. (No answer, pp. 106–107)
38. (No answer)

Controlling the Voice *18*

TRUE/FALSE QUESTIONS

1. Pitch is the relative loudness of a speaker's voice while giving a speech.

2. The proper volume for delivering a speech is somewhat louder than that of normal conversation.

3. When adjusting speaking volume, a speaker should consider the size of the room and the number of people in the audience.

4. The speaker's mouth should be positioned one to three inches from the microphone.

5. Pitch represents the range of sounds from high to low.

6. When there is no variety in pitch, speaking becomes monotonous.

7. Public speakers should strive to vary the rate of speaking.

8. Novice speakers usually pause for too long a time at dramatic moments in a speech.

9. Unnecessary and undesirable words used to fill pauses are called *vocal fillers.*

10. Volume, pitch, rate, and pauses work independently of each other.

11. Enthusiasm is one key to achieving vocal variety in a speech.

12. A speaker's overexcitement may result in a consistently low pitch.

13. Pronunciation is clarity or forcefulness in saying words so they are audible and discernible.

14. Incorrect pronunciations are often a matter of habit.

15. Articulation problems are much rarer than pronunciation problems and are usually very difficult to overcome.

16. If a speaker tends to mumble, he or she should practice speaking louder and with emphatic pronunciation.

MULTIPLE-CHOICE QUESTIONS

17. The proper volume for delivering a speech depends on which of the following factors?
    A) the size of the room and number of persons in the audience
    B) the availability of a microphone
    C) background noise
    D) all of the above

18. Speakers whose volume is too _____ are viewed less positively than those who project their voices at a pleasing volume.
    A) low
    B) enthusiastic
    C) monotone
    D) fast

19. Pitch is
    A) the relative loudness of a speaker's voice.
    B) the speed at which a speaker talks.
    C) the rate at which a speaker stops and starts.
    D) the range of sounds a speaker's voice produces, from high to low.

20. One key to achieving effective vocal variety is
    A) enthusiasm.
    B) visual aids.
    C) pronunciation.
    D) monotony.

21. Incorrect word pronunciations
    A) are a matter of habit.
    B) distract the audience.
    C) cannot be improved by clear articulation.
    D) are all of the above.

FILL-IN-THE-BLANK QUESTIONS

22. _____ is the relative loudness of a speaker's voice while giving a speech.

23. The proper volume for delivering a speech is somewhat _____ than that of normal conversation.

24. A speaker should adjust the speaking _____ to the size of the room and the number of people in the audience.

25. The speaker's mouth should be positioned about _____ inches from a handheld or fixed microphone.

26. The range of sounds from high to low is known as _____ .

27. Novice speakers are especially uncomfortable with _____ .

28. Unnecessary and undesirable words used to fill pauses are called _____ .

29. Enthusiasm is one key to achieving _____ variety.

ESSAY AND SHORT ANSWER QUESTIONS

30. Explain how a speaker can learn to adjust his or her speaking volume.

31. Identify three tips for using a microphone when delivering a speech.

32. List two ways a speaker can avoid a monotonous speaking style.

33. Give an example of vocal fillers, and explain why they distract from the speech message.

34. What are two things a speaker can do to correct articulation and pronunciation problems?

35. Explain the difference between pronunciation and articulation. Why are these elements of a speaker's vocal delivery so important?

ANSWER KEY FOR CHAPTER 18

1. False (p. 109)
2. True (p. 109)
3. True (p. 109)
4. False (p. 109)
5. True (p. 109)
6. True (p. 109)
7. True (p. 110)
8. False (p. 110)
9. True (p. 110)
10. False (p. 111)
11. True (p. 111)
12. True (p. 111)
13. False (p. 111)
14. True (p. 111)
15. False (p. 111)
16. True (p. 112)
17. D (p. 109)
18. A (p. 109)
19. D (p. 109)
20. A (p. 111)
21. D (p. 111)
22. Volume (p. 108)
23. louder (p. 109)
24. volume (p. 109)
25. six (p. 109)
26. pitch (p. 109)
27. pauses (p. 110)
28. vocal fillers (p. 110)
29. vocal (p. 111)
30. (No answer, p. 109)
31. (No answer, p. 109)
32. (No answer, p. 111)
33. (No answer, p. 110)
34. (No answer, pp. 111–112)
35. (No answer, pp. 111–112)

Using the Body *19*

TRUE/FALSE QUESTIONS

1. Smiling is an effective way for a speaker to build rapport with an audience.

2. A speaker's deadpan facial expression encourages an audience's attention.

3. Hand gestures are the most important gestures in public speaking.

4. Scanning is a technique whereby speakers gaze briefly at all members of the audience.

5. A speaker's gestures should arise from genuine emotions and should conform to the speaker's personality.

6. If space and time allow, a speaker should try to get out from behind the podium and stand with the audience.

7. How a speaker dresses when delivering a speech is unimportant.

8. Practice is not vital to effective delivery.

9. A speaker who focuses on the message makes the speech delivery more natural and confident.

10. Practicing a speech in front of someone and gaining constructive criticism is helpful for speakers.

11. Speakers should avoid tape recording or videotaping rehearsals of the speech.

12. After rehearsing aloud, a speaker will often revise the speaking outline.

13. When rehearsing a speech, the speaker should try to simulate the actual speech setting but should not practice in front of people.

14. When rehearsing a speech, it is not important for the speaker to time the speech.

15. Speaking experts recommend practicing a speech at least five times in its final form.

MULTIPLE-CHOICE QUESTIONS

16. A speaker who uses the scanning technique often employs the "rule of three," which involves
    A) a technique similar to "pick six."
    B) focusing on the three nearest listeners.
    C) choosing three audience members to focus on in three different areas of the room.
    D) reiterating the main points three times during the speech.

17. Which aspect of the body is most important in maintaining the quality of directness in speech delivery?
    A) eye contact   C) gestures
    B) smiling   D) stance

18. Listeners perceive a speaker who slouches as
    A) sloppy, weak, and unfocused.   C) casual and credible.
    B) unqualified yet friendly.   D) both A and B.

19. The first thing an audience notices about a speaker approaching the speaking position is his or her
    A) eye contact.   C) clothing.
    B) smile.   D) hairstyle.

20. The color yellow for a speaker's clothing conveys
    A) a businesslike attitude.   C) friendliness.
    B) credibility.   D) formality.

21. A speaker should avoid using _____ when rehearsing the speech.
    A) a watch   C) a tape recorder
    B) a video recorder   D) none of the above

22. Videotaping _____ practice sessions is most helpful to a speaker.
    A) two   C) five
    B) four   D) at least six

23. When rehearsing a speech, the speaker should
    A) revise the speaking outline.
    B) practice under realistic conditions.
    C) time the speech.
    D) do all of the above.

24. In sum, a speaker should practice a speech at least _____ times in its final form.
    A) two   C) four
    B) three   D) five

FILL-IN-THE-BLANK QUESTIONS

25. _____ is an effective tool for a speaker to build rapport with an audience.

26. _____ is probably the most important nonverbal behavior in public speaking.

27. _____ is a technique used by speakers whereby they gaze briefly at all members of the audience.

28. A speaker's _____ should arise from genuine emotions and should conform to the speaker's personality.

29. _____ is vital to effective delivery.

30. A speaker who focuses on the _____ makes the speech delivery more natural and confident.

31. Practicing a speech in front of _____ is usually a helpful way for a speaker to rehearse a speech.

32. Speaking experts recommend practicing a speech about _____ times in its final form.

ESSAY AND SHORT ANSWER QUESTIONS

33. Explain why a speaker should always avoid a deadpan facial expression.

34. List two tips for using effective facial expressions.

35. List and explain ways a speaker can maintain eye contact with the audience.

36. List two tips for effective gesturing.

37. Why should a speaker avoid standing stiffly behind the podium?

38. What is the best type of attire for a speaker?

39. List two guidelines for a speaker's dress code.

40. Give three ways that a speaker should practice a speech.

ANSWER KEY FOR CHAPTER 19

1. True (p. 113)
2. False (p. 113)
3. False (p. 114)
4. True (p. 114)
5. True (p. 114)
6. True (p. 115)
7. False (p. 115)
8. False (p. 116)
9. True (p. 116)
10. True (p. 117)
11. False (p. 117)
12. True (p. 116)
13. False (p. 117)
14. False (p. 117)

15. True (p. 117)
16. C (p. 114)
17. A (pp. 113–114)
18. A (p. 115)
19. C (p. 115)
20. C (p. 116)
21. D (pp. 116–117)
22. A (p. 117)
23. D (pp. 116–117)
24. D (p. 117)
25. Smiling (p. 113)
26. Eye contact (pp. 113–114)
27. Scanning (p. 114)
28. gestures (p. 115)

29. Practice (p. 116)
30. message (p. 116)
31. another person (p. 117)
32. five (p. 117)
33. (No answer, p. 113)
34. (No answer, p. 113)
35. (No answer, pp. 113–114)
36. (No answer, p. 115)
37. (No answer, p. 115)
38. (No answer, pp. 115–116)
39. (No answer, p. 116)
40. (No answer, p. 117)

TRUE/FALSE QUESTIONS

1. Messages that are visually reinforced are no more believable than those that are only verbalized.

2. Presentation aids include props, models, pictures, graphs, charts, video, audio, and multimedia.

3. The strength of a presentation aid lies in the context in which it is used.

4. Research indicates that people remember about 20 percent of what they hear but more than 50 percent of what they see and hear.

5. Presentation aids should serve as the main source of a speaker's ideas.

6. Presentation aids allow listeners to engage the left side of the brain, the hemisphere that plays an important role in verbal tasks.

7. Using an actual prop — like a snake or a stone — as a presentation aid can help capture the audience's attention and illustrate key points.

8. It is always practical to include props in a presentation.

9. A model is a two-dimensional representation of an object.

10. Because they are economical and easy to use, posters are a good choice for speakers who give the same presentation many times.

11. Line graphs are useful in representing information that changes over time.

12. A pie graph uses bars of varying lengths to compare quantities or magnitudes.

13. To show the sequence of activities or the directional flow in a process, the pictogram is the visual aid of choice.

14. Video can be a powerful presentation aid combining sight, sound, and movement to illustrate key speech concepts.

15. Multimedia combines several media into a single production.

16. The use of multimedia helps people learn and master information more quickly than they would by conventional means.

17. Generating and designing presentation aids by hand is a more popular choice for contemporary speakers than is using the computer.

18. One disadvantage of using overhead transparencies is that they must be shown in a darkened room.

19. The video projector is one of the most common presentation media.

20. Projection devices that use LCD technology for displaying information come in two forms: the LCD panel and the LCD projector.

21. Video projectors, LCD panels, and LCD projectors are excellent technological presentation aids for large audiences.

22. Flip charts are good presentation aids for speakers with few artistic skills.

23. Handouts used for presentation aids should always be passed out before a speech begins.

MULTIPLE-CHOICE QUESTIONS

24. In Russell's speech about his hobby as an amateur taxidermist, he exhibited several mounted animals as his presentation aids. Which type of presentation aid did Russell use?
    A) models
    B) props
    C) pictograms
    D) handouts

25. Pictures as presentation aids include
    A) diagrams.
    B) maps.
    C) posters.
    D) all of the above.

26. Which type of graph is useful for presenting information that changes over time?
    A) bar graph
    B) line graph
    C) pie graph
    D pictogram

27. In her speech about divorce rates, Geneva wanted to show a comparison of divorce rates among three states. In order to best illustrate these comparisons, Geneva used a
    A) bar graph.
    B) flowchart.
    C) pie graph.
    D) pictogram.

28. Which type of chart illustrates the sequence of activities or the directional flow in a process?
    A) flowchart
    B) organizational chart
    C) pictogram
    D) table

29. When constructing a pictogram, the speaker should
    A) select pictures that are different from one another.
    B) make sure the pictures contrast in size and shape.
    C) be certain that the pictorial representation will be understood by viewers.
    D) do all of the above.

30. When using audio or video as a presentation aid, the speaker should be sure to
    A) check to see if the material is copyrighted.
    B) cue the tape before the presentation.
    C) tell the audience what they will hear or see beforehand and discuss its significance afterward.
    D) do all of the above.

31. As a presentation aid, multimedia
    A) cannot yet utilize the Internet.
    B) currently has only two presentation graphics programs from which to choose.
    C) helps visual but not auditory reinforcement of information.
    D) is more time consuming to prepare than conventional presentation aids.

FILL-IN-THE-BLANK QUESTIONS

32. _____ aids are visual or auditory elements used by a speaker that include props, models, pictures, graphs, charts, video, audio, and multimedia.

33. A(n) _____ is a three-dimensional, scale-size representation of an object.

34. A(n) _____ represents numerical data in visual form.

35. A diagram that shows a step-by-step progression through a procedure, relationship, or process is called a(n) _____ .

36. A(n) _____ graph uses columns of various lengths to compare quantities or magnitudes.

37. When creating line and bar graphs, a speaker should put no more than _____ lines of data on one graph.

38. A graph should always be assigned a clear _____ .

39. When creating a pie graph, the number of pie slices should be restricted to _____ .

40. Video- and audio-_____ are reusable, which makes these media both durable and cost-effective.

41. A presentation aid that combines several media (such as voice, video, text, and data) into a single production is called _____ .

42. An LCD _____ is a device with its own light source that allows a speaker to project what is on a computer screen.

43. Page-size items conveying information that cannot practically be delivered in another manner or that are kept by listeners after the presentation are called _____ .

ESSAY AND SHORT ANSWER QUESTIONS

44. Explain the difference between a line graph and a bar graph.

45. When would a pictogram be more suitable than a bar graph as a presentation aid?

46. What is a pie graph, and when would it be appropriate for use as a presentation aid?

47. List two advantages of using overhead transparencies.

48. Identify two advantages and two disadvantages of using handouts as a presentation aid.

ANSWER KEY FOR CHAPTER 20

1. False (p. 119)	17. False (p. 124)	33. model (p. 119)
2. True (p. 119)	18. False (p. 125)	34. graph (p. 120)
3. True (p. 119)	19. False (p. 125)	35. flowchart (p. 122)
4. True (p. 119)	20. True (p. 125)	36. bar (p. 120)
5. False (p. 119)	21. True (p. 125)	37. two (p. 121)
6. False (p. 119)	22. False (p. 125)	38. title (p. 121)
7. True (p. 119)	23. False (p. 126)	39. seven (p. 121)
8. False (p. 120)	24. B (p. 119)	40. tapes (p. 124)
9. False (p. 119)	25. D (p. 119)	41. multimedia (p. 124)
10. True (p. 126)	26. B (p. 120)	42. projector (p. 125)
11. True (p. 120)	27. A (p. 120)	43. handouts (p. 126)
12. False (p. 121)	28. A (p. 122)	44. (No answer, pp. 120–121)
13. False (p. 121)	29. C (p. 121)	45. (No answer, pp. 120–121)
14. True (p. 124)	30. D (p. 124)	46. (No answer, p. 121)
15. True (p. 124)	31. D (p. 124)	47. (No answer, p. 125)
16. True (p. 124)	32. Presentation (p. 119)	48. (No answer, p. 126)

21 *Designing Presentation Aids*

TRUE/FALSE QUESTIONS

1. A presentation aid with words should have no more than eight words per line.

2. A presentation aid with words should have no more than five lines per aid.

3. Key design elements such as fonts, color, and italics should be consistent with each presentation aid to maintain continuity.

4. Presentation aids that try to communicate too many messages will overwhelm the audience.

5. Limiting the number of words in a presentation aid increases the likelihood that the audience will spend too much time reading the aid rather than listening to the speaker.

6. Each presentation aid should be simple and uncomplicated and should present three major ideas.

7. The word *font* refers to a specific style of lettering.

8. Sans serif typefaces include small flourishes, or strokes, at the tops and bottoms of each letter.

9. Boldface, underlining, and italics should be used sparingly to call attention to the most important points.

10. Presentation aids are most effective when the words are written in all uppercase letters.

11. For on-screen projection, a speaker should not use a font smaller than 18-point text.

12. For on-screen projection, titles or major headings should be 36-point text.

13. For on-screen projection, regular text should be 12-point type.

14. Colors evoke distinct associations in people.

15. Bold, bright colors should be used to emphasize important points.

16. Different audiences may assign different meanings to particular colors.

17. Avoid dark colors for presentation aid backgrounds.

18. Presentation aids that use four or more colors are more effective than those that use only two or three.

19. When using color, stay within the same family of hues.

MULTIPLE-CHOICE QUESTIONS

20. How many major ideas should be present on each presentation aid?
    A) one
    B) two
    C) three
    D) four

21. When designing a presentation aid, the speaker should strive for
    A) simplicity.
    B) abstraction.
    C) complexity.
    D) diversity.

22. Typefaces come in a variety of sizes or
    A) scripts.
    B) sans scripts.
    C) fonts.
    D) serifs.

23. The two categories of typefaces are sans serif and
    A) script.
    B) sans script.
    C) font.
    D) serif.

24. When the body of a text is being read, which typeface is easiest on the eye?
    A) script
    B) sans script
    C) font
    D) serif

25. Small amounts of text, such as headings, are best viewed in which type?
    A) script
    B) sans script
    C) sans serif
    D) serif

26. The typeface or font in a presentation should be
    A) simple.
    B) easy to read.
    C) not distracting.
    D) all of the above.

27. Boldface, underlining, and italics should
    A) be used as often as possible.
    B) emphasize both major and minor points.
    C) be used sparingly.
    D) do both A and B.

28. The skillful use of color in presentation aids can be used to
    A) draw attention to key points.
    B) set the mood of a speech.
    C) do both A and B.
    D) do neither A nor B.

29. The background color of a presentation aid
    A) should be dark.
    B) should have several hues.
    C) should be neutral in color.
    D) should blend into the type.

FILL-IN-THE-BLANK QUESTIONS

30. The principle of _____ states that it is appropriate to present one major idea per aid.

31. The principle of _____ dictates that the same design should apply to all presentation aids displayed in a speech.

32. The purpose of _____ is to reinforce, support, or summarize the speaker's words.

33. A presentation aid with words should have no more than _____ words per line.

34. Key design elements such as fonts, color, and italics should be consistent with each presentation aid to maintain _____ .

35. Presentation aids that try to communicate too many messages will overwhelm the _____ .

36. Limiting the number of _____ in a presentation aid lessens the likelihood that the audience will spend too much time reading the aid rather than listening to the speaker.

37. Different sizes of typefaces are called _____ .

38. The word _____ refers to a specific style of lettering.

39. For on-screen projection, titles or major headings should be in _____ type.

40. For on-screen projection, regular text should be in _____ type.

ESSAY AND SHORT ANSWER QUESTIONS

41. How many major ideas should be presented in each presentation aid? Why?

42. Explain the principle of simplicity and give an example.

43. Give three tips for using typefaces and fonts effectively in a presentation aid.

44. Explain why text in a presentation aid should appear in upper- and lowercase type rather than in all uppercase.

45. List four ways to optimize color in designing presentation aids.

ANSWER KEY FOR CHAPTER 21

1. True (p. 127)
2. False (p. 127)
3. True (p. 127)
4. True (p. 127)
5. False (p. 127)
6. False (p. 127)
7. False (p. 127)
8. False (p. 127)
9. True (p. 128)
10. False (p. 128)
11. True (p. 128)
12. True (p. 128)
13. False (p. 128)
14. True (p. 129)
15. True (p. 129)

16. True (p. 129)
17. True (p. 128)
18. False (p. 130)
19. True (p. 130)
20. A (p. 127)
21. A (p. 127)
22. C (p. 127)
23. D (p. 127)
24. D (p. 128)
25. C (p. 128)
26. D (p. 128)
27. C (p. 128)
28. C (p. 128)
29. C (p. 128)
30. simplicity (p. 127)

31. continuity (p. 127)
32. presentation aids (p. 127)
33. eight (p. 127)
34. continuity (p. 130)
35. audience (p. 127)
36. words (p. 127)
37. fonts (p. 127)
38. typeface (p. 127)
39. 36-point (p. 128)
40. 18-point (p. 128)
41. (No answer, p. 127)
42. (No answer, p. 127)
43. (No answer, p. 128)
44. (No answer, p. 128)
45. (No answer, pp. 128–130)

A Brief Guide to Microsoft PowerPoint **22**

TRUE/FALSE QUESTIONS

1. Presentation software packages offer public speakers powerful tools for creating and displaying professionally polished visual aids.

2. Presentation software allows the user to import video and sound for a multimedia presentation.

3. PowerPoint gives users the ability to modify and revise the aids up to the minute the speech is delivered.

4. With PowerPoint, a speaker can generate slides containing text, artwork, and photos, but not video or sound.

5. In PowerPoint, a touch screen allows quick access to the most frequently used program functions.

6. In PowerPoint, a dialog box allows the user to choose how he or she will create a new presentation or revise an existing one.

7. In PowerPoint, transition effects add special motion and sound effects as the user moves from one slide to another.

8. Animation effects are also referred to as *builds*.

9. PowerPoint 2000 comes with either Preset or Custom animations.

10. With PowerPoint, clip art cannot be imported from other online programs.

11. Technology should not get in the way of a speaker's relating to the audience.

MULTIPLE-CHOICE QUESTIONS

12. Which of the following options does PowerPoint offer for creating a new presentation?
    A) AutoFixer
    B) AutoContent Wizard
    C) AutoPlanning
    D) all of the above

13. Which of the following PowerPoint options offers the greatest degree of help?
    A) AutoContent Wizard
    B) Template option
    C) Blank Presentation option
    D) Guidebook Pattern

14. Which of the following PowerPoint options is best for speakers who want more flexibility in designing their graphics?
    A) AutoContent Wizard
    B) Template option
    C) Blank Presentation option
    D) Guidebook Pattern

15. Which of the following PowerPoint options allows you to select the layout and color scheme for each slide in your presentation?
    A) AutoContent Wizard
    B) Template option
    C) Blank Presentation option
    D) Guidebook Pattern

16. In which mode of PowerPoint do users customize every aspect of the presentation?
    A) AutoContent Wizard
    B) Template option
    C) Blank Presentation option
    D) Guidebook Pattern

17. Which of the following PowerPoint options allows the greatest degree of creativity and flexibility?
    A) AutoContent Wizard
    B) Template option
    C) Blank Presentation option
    D) Guidebook Pattern

18. Which view in PowerPoint allows the user to look at one entire slide on the screen and edit it?
    A) normal view
    B) outline view
    C) slide sorter view
    D) slide show view

19. Which view in PowerPoint provides a graphical representation of all the slides in the presentation?
    A) slide view
    B) outline view
    C) slide sorter view
    D) slide show view

20. Which view in PowerPoint is meant to be used during projection to an audience?
    A) slide view
    B) outline view
    C) slide sorter view
    D) slide show view

21. Used sparingly, which of the following PowerPoint effects can add to the effectiveness of a presentation?
    A) transitions
    B) animations
    C) both A and B
    D) neither A nor B

22. Which of the following can be inserted into PowerPoint slides?
    A) clip art
    B) charts
    C) tables and worksheets
    D) all of the above

FILL-IN-THE-BLANK QUESTIONS

23. The three options for creating a new presentation in PowerPoint are _____ , _____ , and _____ .

24. For every graphic the user creates, PowerPoint creates a set of _____ .

25. In PowerPoint, _____ effects add special motion and sound effects as the user moves from one slide to another.

26. Animation effects are also referred to as _____ .

27. With PowerPoint 2000, the user can insert tables and _____ into a slide.

ESSAY AND SHORT ANSWER QUESTIONS

28. Identify three components of PowerPoint's AutoContent Wizard option.

29. Under what circumstances might a speaker choose PowerPoint's Template option for designing presentation aids?

30. When should a speaker choose PowerPoint's Blank Presentation option?

31. Explain how PowerPoint's "masters" aid the speaker in preparing presentation aids.

32. Define *animation effects* and explain their use in PowerPoint.

33. List two objects that can be created or imported into PowerPoint slides.

34. Give three tips for successfully incorporating electronic presentations into a speech.

ANSWER KEY FOR CHAPTER 22

1. True (p. 130)

2. True (p. 130)

3. True (p. 130)

4. False (p. 130)

5. False (p. 130)

6. True (p. 131)

7. True (p. 135)

8. True (p. 135)

9. False (p. 135)

10. False (p. 137)

11. True (p. 138)

12. B (p. 131)

13. A (p. 131)

14. B (p. 133)

15. B (p. 133)

16. C (p. 133)

17. C (p. 133)

18. A (p. 133)

19. C (p. 133)

20. D (p. 135)

21. C (p. 136)

22. D (p. 137)

23. AutoContent Wizard; Design Template option; Blank Presentation option (p. 131)

24. masters (p. 135)

25. transition (p. 135)

26. builds (p. 135)

27. worksheets (p. 137)

28. (No answer, p. 131)

29. (No answer, p. 133)

30. (No answer, p. 133)

31. (No answer, p. 135)

32. (No answer, p. 135)

33. (No answer, pp. 136–137)

34. (No answer, p. 138)

Informative Speaking 23

TRUE/FALSE QUESTIONS

1. The goal of informative speaking is to persuade or convince an audience.

2. Selecting an appropriate organizational pattern aids audience comprehension of a speech.

3. The audience is an empty vessel into which a speaker can pour facts and figures.

4. An understanding of the audience and the factors affecting them is insignificant in delivering an effective informative speech.

5. When preparing an informative speech, a speaker should focus exclusively on what he or she believes listeners should know by the end of the speech.

6. In an informative speech, the speaker is allowed to describe or explain but not demonstrate.

7. Operational definitions define something by describing what it does.

8. Definition by etymology describes something by explaining what it is not.

9. Definition by synonym defines something by providing examples of the subject under discussion.

10. *Etymology* is a term for the comparison of a word with its opposite.

11. In describing information, the speaker should provide an array of details so as to allow the audience to paint a mental picture of the topic.

12. The point of a speech of explanation is to offer a vivid portrayal of the subject under discussion.

13. Speeches that rely on demonstration often work with the actual object, models of it, or visual aids that diagram it.

14. Speeches about events focus on noteworthy occurrences, both past and present.

15. By relating new ideas to old ones, a speaker enables listeners to better understand the information they are given.

16. Visualization is a descriptive way to ensure the audience's grasp of a topic.

17. People process and retain information best when it is presented in only one format.

18. To assist audience members in retaining information from your speech, it is helpful to tell them in the introduction what you hope they will learn by listening to you.

19. If the speaker guides the audience toward grasping the topic's relevance gradually throughout the course of a speech, the audience will become more emotionally attached to the topic and to the speech's outcome.

MULTIPLE-CHOICE QUESTIONS

20. An informative speaker might introduce listeners to
   A) ideas or events.
   B) people or processes.
   C) neither A nor B.
   D) both A and B.

21. The goal of informative speaking is
   A) to decrease audience frustration and boredom.
   B) to influence attitudes, beliefs, values, and behaviors.
   C) to increase audience understanding and awareness.
   D) all of the above.

22. Defining one term by comparing it to another term that has an equivalent meaning is called
   A) definition by synonym.   C) definition by etymology.
   B) operational definition.   D) none of the above.

23. Defining, describing, demonstrating, and explaining are all related to
   A) persuasive speaking.   C) informative speaking.
   B) entertaining speaking.   D) demonstrative speaking.

24. A definition by word origin is called
   A) definition by synonym.   C) definition by etymology.
   B) operational definition.   D) definition by negation.

25. Speeches about _____ inform audiences about historically significant individuals and groups.
   A) people   C) objects
   B) events   D) processes

26. Speeches about _____ discuss anything that is not human.
    A) people   C) objects
    B) events   D) processes

27. Speeches about _____ refer to a series of steps that lead to a finished product or end result.
    A) people   C) objects
    B) events   D) processes

28. Speeches about _____ present a matter in dispute in order to increase understanding and awareness.
    A) concepts   C) objects
    B) issues   D) processes

29. Speeches about _____ discuss abstract or complex ideas and attempt to make them concrete and understandable.
    A) concepts   C) objects
    B) issues   D) processes

30. Grayson delivered an informative speech on romantic relationships. He described the stages of relationship formation, how partners interact, why miscommunication occurs, how people change in relationships, and the effects of jealousy and suspicion on a relationship's stability. Because the speech was too long, the audience became bored. From this description, what was Grayson's mistake?
    A) poor topic selection
    B) incoherent organization
    C) lack of appropriate research
    D) including too much information

31. One of the simplest and most effective ways to reinforce new information in an informative speech is to
    A) mention the new topic only in the beginning of the speech.
    B) repeat key words or phrases about that information.
    C) repeat key words only in the introduction and conclusion.
    D) relate new ideas to unfamiliar ideas.

32. To describe information, a speaker should use language that
    A) concise.   C) vivid.
    B) concrete.   D) all of the above.

FILL-IN-THE-BLANK QUESTIONS

33. To _____ is to communicate knowledge.

34. The goal of informative speaking is to increase the understanding and awareness of your _____ by imparting knowledge.

35. Definition by _____ defines something by explaining what it is not.

36. A(n) _____ definition defines something by explaining what it does.

37. Definition by _____ compares one term to another with an equivalent meaning.

38. The origin of a word is its _____ .

39. Speeches about _____ focus on noteworthy occurrences, both past and present.

40. Speeches about _____ refer to a series of steps that lead to an end result.

41. Speeches about _____ provide an overview of problems in order to increase understanding and awareness.

42. A speaker can simply and effectively reinforce new information by using _____ .

ESSAY AND SHORT ANSWER QUESTIONS

43. List three ways a speaker can build audience awareness and understanding in an informative speech.

44. Name three ways a speaker can define information, and give an example of each.

45. How is explaining information different from describing information?

46. Provide an example of a speech topic that would be appropriate for demonstrating information.

47. List the subject matter categories of informative speeches.

48. List three guidelines for presenting effective informative speeches.

ANSWER KEY FOR CHAPTER 23

1. False (p. 140)	17. False (p. 143)	33. inform (p. 140)
2. True (p. 143)	18. True (p. 144)	34. audience (p. 140)
3. False (p. 143)	19. False (p. 143)	35. negation (p. 142)
4. False (p. 140)	20. D (pp. 140–141)	36. operational (p. 142)
5. False (p. 140)	21. C (p. 140)	37. synonym (p. 142)
6. False (p. 142)	22. A (p. 142)	38. etymology (p. 142)
7. True (p. 142)	23. C (pp. 141–142)	39. events (p. 140)
8. False (p. 142)	24. C (p. 142)	40. processes (p. 141)
9. False (p. 142)	25. A (p. 140)	41. issues (p. 141)
10. False (p. 142)	26. C (p. 140)	42. repetition (p. 145)
11. True (p. 142)	27. D (p. 141)	43. (No answer, pp. 144–145)
12. False (p. 142)	28. B (p. 141)	44. (No answer, p. 142)
13. True (p. 142)	29. A (p. 141)	45. (No answer, p. 142)
14. True (p. 140)	30. D (p. 145)	46. (No answer, p. 142)
15. True (p. 145)	31. B (p. 145)	47. (No answer, pp. 140–141)
16. True (p. 145)	32. D (p. 145)	48. (No answer, pp. 144–146)

24 *Persuasive Speaking*

TRUE/FALSE QUESTIONS

1. The general goal of persuasive speeches is to increase understanding and awareness.

2. All persuasive speeches explicitly seek a response from the audience.

3. Persuasive appeals directed at the audience's reasoning on a topic are termed logos.

4. Pathos involves the appeal to audience emotion.

5. According to Aristotle, appealing to the emotions of the listeners is called ethos.

6. One element of an ethos-based appeal is the speaker's moral character.

7. Maslow's hierarchy of needs is a set of ten basic human needs.

8. The highest level in Maslow's hierarchy is self-esteem needs.

9. Visualization is the fourth step in Monroe's motivated sequence pattern.

10. In the refutation organizational pattern, each main point addresses and then disproves an opposing claim.

11. An argument is a stated position with support either for or against an idea or issue.

12. A claim states the speaker's conclusion, based on evidence.

13. Material that provides grounds for belief in a claim is called evidence.

14. External evidence can be thought of as supporting material.

15. Narratives, testimony, and facts drawn from an outside source are examples of external evidence.

MULTIPLE-CHOICE QUESTIONS

16. A persuasive speech
    A) attempts to influence audience choices.
    B) presents listeners with a limited number of alternatives to consider.
    C) seeks a response from the audience.
    D) does all of the above.

17. Under which of the following conditions is the persuasive purpose appropriate?
    A) when you seek to expand an audience's alternatives
    B) when you seek to change an audience's behavior
    C) when you seek to reinforce an audience's attitudes, beliefs, or behavior
    D) both B and C

18. The appeal to audience emotion is termed
    A) logos.   C) pathos.
    B) ethos.   D) credos.

19. In his persuasive speech about why people should buy used rather than new autos, Maverick provided the audience with convincing information due to his knowledge and experience as a used-car salesperson. Maverick employed which type of appeal?
    A) logos   C) pathos
    B) ethos   D) credos

20. Buck gave a persuasive speech about why people should assist the homeless in his city in order to prevent crime. According to Maslow, this speech appealed to which basic need?
    A) physiological   C) social
    B) safety   D) self-esteem

21. In his presentation, Kyle encouraged his colleagues to reach their highest potential and take pride in their work. According to Maslow's hierarchy, which need did Kyle appeal to?
    A) physiological   C) self-esteem
    B) social   D) self-actualization

22. According to the Elaboration Likelihood Model, more long-lasting changes in audience perspectives occur if listeners process the speech message
    A) centrally.   C) favorably.
    B) peripherally.   D) diffusively.

23. The audience's perceptions of and attitudes toward a speaker make up the speaker's
    A) expertise.   C) ethos.
    B) credibility.   D) persuasiveness.

24. Claims of policy fit naturally into which organizational pattern?
    A) problem-solution   C) cause-effect
    B) refutation   D) comparative advantage

25. Which organizational pattern addresses main points and then disproves opposing claims?
    A) problem-solution   C) cause-effect
    B) refutation   D) comparative advantage

26. Which pattern demonstrates how the speaker's points are more favorable than alternative positions?
    A) problem-solution   C) cause-effect
    B) refutation   D) comparative advantage

27. In persuasive speaking, arguments are created to
    A) change people's opinions.
    B) influence behavior.
    C) justify the speaker's beliefs or actions.
    D) do all of the above.

28. The Chicago Bulls were the best NBA team of the 1990s. This statement is a claim of
    A) value.   C) policy.
    B) fact.   D) none of the above.

29. Students who earn an A average on all speech assignments should be exempt from the final exam. This statement is a claim of
    A) value.   C) policy.
    B) fact.   D) none of the above.

30. To build a strong case for a claim of _____ , the speaker must provide the audience with a three-part justification consisting of a need or problem, a solution, and evidence of the solution's feasibility.
    A) value   C) policy
    B) fact   D) third order

31. The most persuasive kind of evidence is
    A) the audience's knowledge and opinions about the topic.
    B) the speaker's assertions based on personal experience and knowledge.
    C) information from external sources, such as testimony and statistics.
    D) none of the above.

FILL-IN-THE-BLANK QUESTIONS

32. Speech that is intended to influence the beliefs, attitudes, values, and acts of others is called _____ speaking.

33. A speaker who identifies and appeals to the audience's emotions employs the classical persuasive appeal known as _____ .

34. In classical terms, a speaker's moral character is called _____ .

35. A contemporary persuasive model used by speakers and formulated by Abraham Maslow is Maslow's hierarchy of _____ .

36. The _____ pattern is a five-step process for arousing attention and inspiring action.

37. In the motivated sequence pattern, the _____ step isolates and describes the issue to be addressed.

38. In the motivated sequence pattern, the _____ step identifies the solution.

39. In the motivated sequence pattern, the _____ step involves making a direct request to the audience.

40. A(n) _____ is a stated position with support either for or against an idea or issues.

41. Claims of _____ focus on conditions that actually exist, existed in the past, or will exist in the future.

42. Claims of _____ address issues of judgment and try to show why something is right or wrong, good or bad, worthy or unworthy.

43. _____ evidence is any information in support of a claim that originates with sources other than the audience or the speaker.

44. You can also use an audience's knowledge and opinions and your own _____ as evidence for your claims.

45. A false or erroneous statement, or an invalid or deceptive line of reasoning, is called a logical _____ .

46. An attack on the opponent instead of the opponent's arguments is called a(n) _____ argument.

ESSAY AND SHORT ANSWER QUESTIONS

47. Explain two differences between informative and persuasive speeches.

48. Define and briefly explain the terms logos, ethos, and pathos.

49. How do the audience's perceptions of the speaker's moral character affect the outcome of a persuasive speech?

50. Explain how Maslow's hierarchy of needs relates to persuasive speaking.

51. Discuss specific strategies a speaker could use with a hostile audience.

52. Discuss specific strategies a speaker could use with a sympathetic audience.

53. Describe the steps in Monroe's motivated sequence pattern.

54. Give an example of a speech that uses the comparative advantage arrangement.

55. Give an example of a claim of value.

56. Give an example of a claim of policy.

57. Provide three examples of external evidence.

58. List two reasons why it is important to be able to identify fallacious reasoning.

59. Give an example of the logical fallacy called begging the question.

60. Give an example of an either-or fallacy.

ANSWER KEY FOR CHAPTER 24

1. False (p. 151)
2. False (p. 151)
3. True (p. 152)
4. True (p. 152)
5. False (p. 153)
6. True (p. 153)
7. False (pp. 154–155)
8. False (p. 154)
9. True (p. 163)
10. True (p. 165)
11. True (p. 152)
12. True (p. 156)
13. True (p. 156)
14. True (p. 158)
15. True (p. 158)
16. D (p. 151)
17. D (p. 151)
18. C (p. 152)
19. B (p. 153)
20. B (p. 155)

21. D (p. 155)
22. A (p. 155)
23. B (p. 158)
24. A (p. 160)
25. B (p. 165)
26. D (p. 164)
27. D (p. 152)
28. A (p. 157)
29. C (p. 157)
30. C (p. 157)
31. A (p. 158)
32. persuasive (p. 151)
33. pathos (p. 152)
34. ethos (p. 152)
35. needs (p. 154)
36. motivated sequence (p. 161)
37. need (p. 162)
38. satisfaction (p. 162)
39. action (p. 163)
40. argument (p. 152)

41. fact (p. 156)
42. value (p. 157)
43. External (p. 158)
44. audience analysis (p. 158)
45. fallacy (p. 158)
46. ad hominem (p. 159)
47. (No answer, p. 151)
48. (No answer, pp. 152–153)
49. (No answer, p. 153)
50. (No answer, pp. 154–155)
51. (No answer, p. 160)
52. (No answer, p. 160)
53. (No answer, pp. 161–162)
54. (No answer, p. 164)
55. (No answer, p. 157)
56. (No answer, p. 157)
57. (No answer, p. 158)
58. (No answer, p. 158)
59. (No answer, p. 159)
60. (No answer, p. 159)

25 *Speaking on Special Occasions*

TRUE/FALSE QUESTIONS

1. The one underlying function of a special occasion speech is to entertain.

2. Special occasion speeches can be either informative or persuasive.

3. A commemorative special occasion speech is one that might occur at a wedding, anniversary, or retirement party.

4. Special occasion speeches may function to celebrate a person or event.

5. The goal of a speech of introduction is to inspire the audience.

6. A person who delivers a speech of introduction should not mention the speaker's awards, accomplishments, and achievements.

7. The final part of the introducer's task is to talk about herself or himself.

8. The purpose of a speech of acceptance is to express gratitude for the honor bestowed on the speaker.

9. In a speech of acceptance, it is always appropriate for the speaker to say, "I really just don't know what to say."

10. The goals of a speech of presentation are to communicate the meaning of the award and to explain why the recipient is receiving it.

11. A roast is a brief tribute to a person or event being celebrated.

12. A verbal tribute to a deceased person is called a *eulogy*.

13. When delivering a eulogy, the speaker should focus on the life of the person rather than the circumstances of death.

14. In general, an after-dinner speech is expected to be somber and serious.

15. After-dinner speeches always take place after an evening meal.

16. A speaker should usually avoid presenting a stand-up comedy routine during an after-dinner speech.

17. The purpose of an after-dinner speech may be to entertain or set a social agenda.

18. A speech of inspiration attempts to uplift the audience and help them see things in a positive light.

19. Inspirational speeches are rarely used in the business world.

20. A dynamic delivery style is inappropriate for a speech of inspiration.

21. In delivering an inspirational speech, the speaker should make the goal of the speech clear to the audience.

22. Inspirational speeches should be concluded with a dramatic ending.

23. Many successful inspirational speakers use acronyms as devices to organize their speeches.

MULTIPLE-CHOICE QUESTIONS

24. Which of the following is a function of a special occasion speech?
    A) to make a compelling argument
    B) to change an audience's beliefs
    C) to set a social agenda
    D) all of the above

25. Banquets, awards dinners, and roasts are examples of special occasion speeches that usually strive to
    A) commemorate.   C) inspire.
    B) entertain.   D) set a social agenda.

26. Fund-raisers, campaign banquets, conferences, and conventions are examples of special occasion speeches that strive to
    A) commemorate.   C) inspire.
    B) entertain.   D) set a social agenda.

27. Anniversaries of important events and memorial dedications are examples of special occasion speeches that strive to
    A) commemorate.   C) inspire.
    B) entertain.   D) set a social agenda.

28. A speaker who delivers a speech of introduction should avoid
    A) preparing for the speech.
    B) talking briefly.
    C) evaluating or offering critical commentary on the speech of the person being introduced.
    D) all of the above.

29. In a speech of introduction, the introducer's task is to tell the audience something about
    A) the speaker's shortcomings.
    B) the speaker's background.
    C) the speaker's attire.
    D) all of the above.

30. A speaker who has been introduced should respond to the introduction by
    A) acknowledging the introducer.
    B) thanking the introducer.
    C) using a combination of humility and humor.
    D) doing all of the above.

31. The function of a speech of acceptance is to
    A) express gratitude for the honor bestowed.
    B) react with surprise.
    C) question whether the speaker should have been given the award.
    D) describe the speaker's background and accomplishments.

32. For a speech of presentation, the speaker should
    A) assume the audience knows the meaning of the award.
    B) assume the audience knows why the recipient is receiving the award.
    C) plan the actual presentation of the award.
    D) do none of the above.

33. In a speech of presentation, the speaker should
    A) convey the meaning of the award.
    B) identify the sponsors of the award.
    C) explain why the recipient is being honored.
    D) do all of the above.

34. Several of Anne's closest friends celebrated their twenty-year friendship with her by delivering a series of short comical accounts of their relationship with Anne. Which type of special occasion speech did Anne's friends use?
    A) a toast
    B) a roast
    C) a eulogy
    D) an after-dinner speech

35. People with little or no public speaking experience will most likely deliver which type of special occasion speech at some point in their lives?
    A) a toast
    B) a roast
    C) a eulogy
    D) an after-dinner speech

36. When delivering a eulogy, the speaker should be sure to
    A) avoid mentioning the deceased's family.
    B) focus on the circumstances of the death.
    C) show intense grief.
    D) emphasize the deceased's positive qualities.

37. President John F. Kennedy's inaugural address, in which he challenged Americans, "Ask not what your country can do for you, but what you can do for your country," is an example of a
    A) speech of introduction.   C) eulogy.
    B) speech of inspiration.   D) speech of acceptance.

38. Examples of ordinary people who triumph over adversity and achieve extraordinary dreams are often used in a
    A) speech of introduction.   C) eulogy.
    B) speech of inspiration.   D) speech of acceptance.

39. One of the most successful strategies a speaker can use in inspirational speaking is
    A) memorizing the speech.
    B) using charts and graphs.
    C) incorporating hypothetical examples.
    D) employing a dynamic speaking style.

FILL-IN-THE-BLANK QUESTIONS

40. The function of a(n) _____ speech is to entertain, celebrate, commemorate, inspire, or set a social agenda.

41. Banquets, awards dinners, and roasts are examples of special occasion speeches that have as their purpose to _____ .

42. A speech of _____ is a short speech that prepares the audience for another speaker and motivates them to listen.

43. In a speech of _____ , the recipient expresses gratitude for the honor bestowed on him or her and acknowledges others who have contributed to his or her success.

44. In a speech of _____ , the speaker communicates the importance of the award and explains why the recipient is receiving it.

45. A type of special occasion speech that is a brief tribute to a person or event being celebrated is referred to as a(n) _____ .

46. A type of special occasion speech that is a humorous tribute to a person, one in which a series of speakers poke fun at him or her, is called a(n) _____ .

47. A(n) _____ is a tribute to a deceased person.

48. A lighthearted and entertaining speech delivered before, during, or after a meal is called a(n) _____ speech.

49. A speech of _____ seeks to uplift the audience and help them see things in a positive light.

ESSAY AND SHORT ANSWER QUESTIONS

50. Discuss three functions of a speech of introduction.

51. How does a speech of acceptance differ from a speech of presentation?

52. Why is it important for a speech of introduction to be brief?

53. List two tips for making a speech of acceptance.

54. What are the goals of a speech of presentation?

55. Explain the difference between a roast and a toast.

56. Name two things a speaker should concentrate on when delivering a eulogy.

57. What is the general purpose of an after-dinner speech?

58. Give an example of a speech of inspiration.

59. Give an example of using an acronym to organize an inspirational speech.

ANSWER KEY FOR CHAPTER 25

1. False (p. 170)	21. True (p. 174)	41. entertain (p. 170)
2. True (p. 170)	22. True (p. 174)	42. introduction (p. 170)
3. False (p. 170)	23. True (p. 174)	43. acceptance (p. 171)
4. True (p. 170)	24. C (p. 170)	44. presentation (p. 172)
5. False (p. 170)	25. B (p. 170)	45. toast (p. 172)
6. False (pp. 170–171)	26. D (p. 170)	46. roast (p. 172)
7. False (p. 171)	27. A (p. 170)	47. eulogy (p. 173)
8. True (p. 171)	28. C (pp. 170–171)	48. after-dinner (p. 173)
9. False (p. 171)	29. B (pp. 170–171)	49. inspiration (p. 174)
10. True (p. 172)	30. D (p. 171)	50. (No answer, p. 170)
11. False (p. 172)	31. A (p. 171)	51. (No answer, pp. 171–172)
12. True (p. 173)	32. C (p. 172)	52. (No answer, p. 171)
13. True (p. 173)	33. D (p. 172)	53. (No answer, pp. 171–172)
14. False (p. 173)	34. B (p. 172)	54. (No answer, p. 172)
15. False (p. 173)	35. A (p. 171)	55. (No answer, p. 172)
16. True (pp. 173–174)	36. D (p. 173)	56. (No answer, p. 173)
17. True (p. 173)	37. B (p. 174)	57. (No answer, p. 173)
18. True (p. 174)	38. B (p. 174)	58. (No answer, p. 174)
19. False (p. 174)	39. D (p. 174)	59. (No answer, p. 174)
20. False (p. 174)	40. special occasion (p. 170)	

26 Typical Classroom Presentation Formats

TRUE/FALSE QUESTIONS

1. Students will not usually be expected to speak publicly at college.

2. A poster session presents information about a study or an issue concisely and visually for an audience at a eulogy.

3. A debate is a type of oral presentation format in which two individuals or groups argue the issue in question from opposing viewpoints.

4. In preparing a poster session presentation, the speaker should use a standard-size poster board.

5. An amateur or outsider audience is a group of people who possess intimate knowledge of the topic or idea being discussed.

6. When presenting to an audience of colleagues within the field, a speaker should always provide background information and definitions.

7. The lay audience has the least amount of knowledge of the given field and topic.

8. Speakers addressing mixed audiences should prepare both detailed and general content.

9. Team presentations and individual presentations share very few characteristics.

10. In team presentations, a strong speaker should be selected to conclude the presentation.

MULTIPLE-CHOICE QUESTIONS

11. College students may be asked to deliver oral presentations in the form of
    A) panel discussions.   C) poster sessions.
    B) team presentations and debates.   D) all of the above.

12. Which of the following is an audience made up of people who possess intimate knowledge of the topic being discussed?
    A) expert   C) lay audience
    B) colleagues within the field   D) mixed audience

13. Which of the following types of audience might comprise academic co-workers, managers, project coordinators, or team leaders?
    A) expert
    B) colleagues within the field
    C) lay audience
    D) mixed audience

14. Which of the following types of audience brings to the presentation the least amount of knowledge of the given topic and field?
    A) expert
    B) colleagues within the field
    C) lay audience
    D) mixed audience

15. Which of the following types of audience consists of people who have expert knowledge along with those who have no specialized knowledge?
    A) expert
    B) colleagues within the field
    C) lay audience
    D) mixed audience

FILL-IN-THE-BLANK QUESTIONS

16. A(n) _____ is an oral presentation prepared and delivered by a group of three or more individuals.

17. A(n) _____ presents information about a study or an issue concisely and visually for participants at professional conferences.

18. A(n) _____ is a type of oral presentation format in which two individuals or groups argue the issue in question from opposing viewpoints.

19. A group of people who possess intimate knowledge of the topic or idea being discussed are referred to as the _____ or insider audience.

20. A(n) _____ audience is one that is unfamiliar with the topic.

21. Speakers addressing _____ audiences should prepare both detailed and general content.

22. A(n) _____ , reasoning, and evidence are all necessary to advance strong arguments in a debate.

ESSAY AND SHORT ANSWER QUESTIONS

23. Why should college students expect to prepare oral presentations in a variety of formats?

24. Compare and contrast the characteristics of team presentations, debates, and poster sessions.

25. Give the characteristics of two types of typical audiences.

26. Identify three necessary components of an oral review of an academic article.

27. List three tips for producing an effective poster session.

28. What is the difference between the expert audience and colleagues within the field?

29. How does a lay audience differ from a mixed audience?

30. List three tips for presenting information to a mixed audience.

ANSWER KEY FOR CHAPTER 26

1. False (p.180)	11. D (p. 180)	21. mixed (p. 181)
2. False (p. 186)	12. A (p. 181)	22. claim (p. 184)
3. True (p. 183)	13. B (p. 181)	23. (No answer, p. 180)
4. True (p. 186)	14. C (p. 181)	24. (No answer, pp. 181–186)
5. False (p. 181)	15. D (p. 181)	25. (No answer, p. 181)
6. False (p. 181)	16. team presentation (p. 181)	26. (No answer, p. 186)
7. True (p. 181)	17. poster sessions (p. 186)	27. (No answer, p. 186)
8. True (p. 181)	18. debate (p. 183)	28. (No answer, p. 181)
9. False (p. 181)	19. expert (p. 181)	29. (No answer, p. 181)
10. True (p. 182)	20. lay (p. 181)	30. (No answer, p. 181)

27 Science and Mathematics Courses

TRUE/FALSE QUESTIONS

1. A panel discussion is an oral presentation prepared and delivered by a group of three or more individuals.

2. Oral presentations in the sciences and mathematics often focus on describing the results of original or replicated research.

3. The purpose of the research overview presentation is to provide context and background for a research question or hypothesis that will form the basis of an impending study.

4. A methods/procedure presentation is typically a thirty-minute group presentation.

5. In many science and mathematical presentations, audience members will expect experimental evidence and mathematical proofs.

6. Scientific and statistical information is not made more comprehensible by illustrating it visually.

7. A successful scientific presentation includes an informative title.

8. In an original research presentation you should clearly state your research question.

9. Research overview presentations are often delivered as a panel discussion.

10. Observation, proofs, and experiments are not necessary in a field study presentation.

MULTIPLE-CHOICE QUESTIONS

11. Science courses include those related to which sciences?
    A) physical
    B) natural
    C) earth
    D) all of the above

12. The _____ presentation for science and math describes original research that the speaker has conducted.
    A) research
    B) field study
    C) research overview
    D) all of the above

13. The purpose of the _____ presentation is to provide content and background for a research question or hypothesis.
    A) research
    B) field study
    C) research overview
    D) methods/procedure

14. The _____ presentation is an informative speech that describes a process.
    A) research
    B) field study
    C) research overview
    D) methods/procedure

15. The _____ presentation describes original research that you have done, either alone or as part of a team.
    A) original research
    B) field study
    C) research overview
    D) methods/procedure

FILL-IN-THE-BLANK QUESTIONS

16. Oral presentations in the _____ often focus on describing the results of original or replicated research.

17. A geology student reporting on a dig is an example of an extended research or _____ presentation.

18. The purpose of the _____ presentation is to provide context and background for a research question or hypothesis that will form the basis of an impending study.

19. A(n) _____ describes original research you have done, either alone or as part of a team.

20. A(n) _____ presentation describes how an experimental or mathematical process works and under what conditions it can be used.

21. In an original research presentation you describe the research question or issue and the scope of the study in the _____ of the speech.

22. In the _____ section of the original research presentation you should highlight the answers to the questions or hypotheses investigated.

23. The _____ presentation can be delivered individually, in teams, or in poster-session format.

24. Research overview presentations are often delivered as a _____ , with several individuals exploring specific lines of research.

ESSAY AND SHORT ANSWER QUESTIONS

25. How is a methods/procedure presentation different from a field study presentation?

26. Provide examples of three types of presentations for science and mathematics.

27. How can a speaker effectively evaluate his or her original research presentation?

28. What three things are described in a methods/procedure presentation?

29. What details are included in a field study presentation?

30. List three tips for preparing a successful scientific presentation.

ANSWER KEY FOR CHAPTER 27

1. False (p. 189)

2. True (p. 187)

3. True (p. 189)

4. False (p. 188)

5. True (p. 190)

6. False (p. 190)

7. True (p. 190)

8. True (p. 188)

9. True (p. 189)

10. False (p. 190)

11. D (p. 187)

12. A (p. 187)

13. C (p. 189)

14. D (p. 188)

15. A (p. 187)

16. sciences and math (p. 187)

17. field study (p. 189)

18. research overview (p. 189)

19. original research presentation (p. 187)

20. methods/procedure (p. 188)

21. introduction (p. 188)

22. results (p. 188)

23. extended research or field study (p. 189)

24. panel discussion (p. 189)

25. (No answer, pp. 188–189)

26. (No answer, pp. 187–189)

27. (No answer, p. 188)

28. (No answer, pp. 188–189)

29. (No answer, p. 189)

30. (No answer, p. 190)

28 *Technical Courses*

1. Oral presentations in technical courses often relate to a current project rather than to prior research.

2. In the request for funding presentation, a member or team provides evidence that a project, proposal, or design is worth funding.

3. The request for funding presentation usually begins with a list of specific reasons a particular project or idea should be funded.

4. A design review provides information on the results of a design project.

5. A prototype is often used in request for funding presentations.

6. In technical presentations you should gear information at a level appropriate to the audience.

7. Technical disciplines include engineering fields, computer-science-oriented fields, and design-oriented fields.

8. In a design review presentation it is not necessary to include a discussion of marketing and economic issues.

9. The request for funding presentation can be delivered as an individual or a team presentation.

10. In technical presentations it is important to begin the speech talking about the results first.

11. When giving a technical presentation it is not necessary to use a visual aid.

12. When giving a technical report to a mixed audience you should find out as much information as you can about the audience.

13. A request for funding presentation is an example of an informative speech.

14. The focus of technical presentations usually rests on the product or design itself.

MULTIPLE-CHOICE QUESTIONS

15. The focus of _____ presentations is often a project the speaker is working on.
    - A) science and math
    - B) social science
    - C) technical
    - D) education

16. Which type of presentation provides evidence that a project, proposal, or design idea is worthy of financial support?
    - A) design review
    - B) technical
    - C) request for funding
    - D) policy recommendation

17. Effective presentations in the technical disciplines are
    - A) detailed and specific in the use of experimental results.
    - B) detailed and specific in the use of numbers.
    - C) detailed and specific in the use of evidence.
    - D) all of the above.

FILL-IN-THE-BLANK QUESTIONS

18. In the _____ presentation, a team member or the entire team provides evidence that a project, proposal, or design is worth funding.

19. A _____ is a model of the design used in a design review.

20. The _____ provides information on the results of a design project.

21. An audience composed of a combination of people—some with expert knowledge and others with no specialized knowledge—is a _____ .

22. _____ is an example of a technical discipline.

23. In order to present a technical report to a mixed audience, you should devote _____ of your time to an overview of your subject and save highly technical material for the remaining time.

24. _____ , such as diagrams, prototypes, and drawings, are often used in technical presentations.

ESSAY AND SHORT ANSWER QUESTIONS

25. Name two types of technical disciplines.

26. How is a design review presentation organized?

27. How is a request for funding presentation organized?

28. Name two types of technical presentations.

29. Identify two characteristics of an effective technical presentation.

30. What can you do to present a technical report to a mixed audience?

ANSWER KEY FOR CHAPTER 28

1. True (p. 191)
2. True (p. 192)
3. False (p. 192)
4. True (p. 191)
5. False (p. 191)
6. True (p. 192)
7. True (p. 191)
8. False (p. 191)
9. True (p. 192)
10. True (p. 192)

11. False (p. 193)
12. True (p. 193)
13. False (p. 192)
14. True (p. 191)
15. C (p. 191)
16. C (p. 192)
17. D (p. 193)
18. request for funding (p. 192)
19. prototype (p. 191)
20. design review (p. 191)

21. mixed audience (pp. 192–193)
22. Computer science (p. 191)
23. one-half to two-thirds (p. 193)
24. Visual aids (p. 193)
25. (No answer, p. 191)
26. (No answer, p. 191)
27. (No answer, p. 192)
28. (No answer, pp. 191–192)
29. (No answer, pp. 192–193)
30. (No answer, p. 193)

29 *Social Science Courses*

TRUE/FALSE QUESTIONS

1. Social scientists conduct qualitative as well as quantitative research.

2. A social science presentation differs from other types of presentations because it focuses on connecting research results with predicting or explaining human behavior or social forces.

3. The types of presentations delivered in science courses are different from presentations delivered in social science courses.

4. The explanatory research presentation reports on studies that attempt to analyze and explain a phenomenon.

5. Social scientists never measure the effectiveness of programs developed to address social issues.

6. The review of the literature presentation reviews the body of research related to a given topic and offers conclusions about the topic based on this research.

7. In a policy recommendation presentation, the audience is a lay audience whose members usually have a vested interest in the problem but are unfamiliar with the intricacies of the field.

8. When social science students participate in a debate, they are never asked to advocate a position they do not support.

9. An effective social science presentation must make use of timely data.

10. A policy recommendation report should begin with recommendations to solve the problem.

11. In quantitative research the emphasis is on observing, describing, and interpreting behavior.

MULTIPLE-CHOICE QUESTIONS

12. Which type of presentation measures the effectiveness of programs?
    A) explanatory research
    B) evaluation research
    C) review of the literature
    D) policy recommendation

13. Which type of presentation describes available research on a topic?
    A) explanatory research
    B) evaluation research
    C) review of the literature
    D) policy recommendation

14. Which type of presentation reports on studies that attempt to analyze and explain a phenomenon?
    A) explanatory research
    B) evaluation research
    C) review of the literature
    D) policy recommendation

15. Which type of presentation offers advice and suggestions on a current issue or problem?
    A) explanatory research
    B) evaluation research
    C) review of the literature
    D) policy recommendation

FILL-IN-THE-BLANK QUESTIONS

16. _____ scientists conduct qualitative research as well as quantitative research.

17. The _____ presentation reports on studies that attempt to analyze and explain a phenomenon.

18. The _____ presentation reviews the body of research related to a given topic and offers conclusions about the topic based on this research.

19. In _____ research the emphasis is on observing, describing, and interpreting behavior.

20. _____ research emphasizes statistical measurement.

21. Social scientists often measure the effectiveness of programs developed to address issues, known as a(n) _____ presentation.

22. A policy recommendation report is typically delivered to a _____ audience.

23. A(n) _____ is used to offer advice and recommendations on a current issue or problem.

ESSAY AND SHORT ANSWER QUESTIONS

24. What is included in a policy recommendation report?

25. What is included in a review of the literature presentation?

26. What is the difference between qualitative and quantitative research?

27. Name two types of social science presentations.

28. Name two ways you can define and explain research.

29. What is included in an evaluation research report?

30. Identify two characteristics of an effective social science presentation.

ANSWER KEY FOR CHAPTER 29

1. True (p. 194)

2. True (p. 194)

3. False (p. 194)

4. True (p. 195)

5. False (p. 195)

6. True (pp. 194–195)

7. True (pp. 195–196)

8. False (p. 194)

9. True (p. 196)

10. False (p. 196)

11. False (p. 194)

12. B (p. 195)

13. C (p. 195)

14. A (p. 195)

15. D (pp. 195–196)

16. Social (p. 194)

17. explanatory research (p. 195)

18. review of the literature (p. 194)

19. qualitative (p. 194)

20. Quantitative (p. 194)

21. evaluation research (p. 195)

22. lay (p. 195)

23. policy recommendation report (p. 195)

24. (No answer, p. 196)

25. (No answer, p. 195)

26. (No answer, p. 194)

27. (No answer, pp. 194–195)

28. (No answer, p. 194)

29. (No answer, p. 195)

30. (No answer, p. 196)

30 Arts and Humanities Courses

TRUE/FALSE QUESTIONS

1. Speaking assignments in the arts and humanities often require the speaker to interpret the meaning of a particular idea, event, person, story, or artifact.

2. Oral presentations in the arts and humanities include informative speeches of explanation, classroom discussions, and debates.

3. Often in arts and humanities, students prepare persuasive speeches.

4. Types of presentations for the arts and humanities most commonly include lectures and group activities.

5. Presentations in the arts and humanities often focus on quantitative research.

6. Visual aids are not necessary when giving presentations in an arts and humanities course.

7. Instructors in the arts and humanities often ask students to compare and contrast events, stories, people, or artifacts.

8. Often students will engage in debates on opposing ideas, historical figures, or philosophical positions.

9. Many students taking arts and humanities courses must research a question and then lead a classroom discussion on it.

10. Effective presentations in the arts and humanities require facts as evidence and leave no room for interpretation.

MULTIPLE-CHOICE QUESTIONS

11. In the arts and humanities, an informative speech of explanation
    A) would never discuss a philosophical school of thought.
    B) always focuses on historical events.
    C) might explain a piece of literature, art, or music.
    D) usually deals with political leaders.

12. Effective presentations in the arts and humanities help the audience to think of the topic in a new way by providing a(n) _____ of/on the topic.
    A) overview   C) interpretation
    B) debate   D) all of the above

13. Sample presentations for education courses include
    A) lectures.   C) classroom discussions.
    B) group activities.   D) all of the above.

14. An effective presentation in education should
    A) always have a logical organization.
    B) separate presentation content and overall course content.
    C) ignore audience-relevant examples, evidence, and support.
    D) always have a chronological organization.

15. What is included in a presentation that compares and contrasts?
    A) thesis statement   C) discussion of main points
    B) concluding evaluative statement   D) all of the above

FILL-IN-THE-BLANK QUESTIONS

16. Speaking assignments in the _____ often require the speaker to interpret the meaning of a particular idea, event, person, story, or artifact.

17. Often in the arts and humanities students prepare _____ speeches.

18. _____ , such as reproductions and photographs, are used in informative speeches of explanation.

19. In a presentation that compares and contrasts, the _____ outlines the connection between the events, stories, people, or artifacts.

20. In a presentation that compares and contrasts, the _____ includes several examples that highlight similarities or differences.

21. In a _____ , the speaker must present a brief assertion about the topic and the opposing speaker then responds with a position.

22. Oral presentations in the arts and humanities include informative speeches of explanation, _____ , and debates.

23. Presentations in the arts and humanities often focus on _____ research.

ESSAY AND SHORT ANSWER QUESTIONS

24. Name two types of arts and humanities presentations.

25. Name three types of arts and humanities courses.

26. What are the three organizational elements for a presentation that compares and contrasts?

27. In a presentation that compares and contrasts, what is the goal of the thesis statement?

28. In a presentation that compares and contrasts, what is included in the discussion of main points?

29. What is included at the end of a presentation that compares and contrasts?

30. Identify two characteristics of an effective arts and humanities presentation.

ANSWER KEY FOR CHAPTER 30

1. True (p. 196)
2. True (p. 197)
3. False (p. 197)
4. False (p. 197)
5. False (p. 197)
6. False (p. 197)
7. True (p. 197)
8. True (p. 198)
9. True (p. 198)
10. False (p. 198)

11. C (p. 197)
12. C (p. 197)
13. D (p. 198)
14. A (p. 198)
15. D (p. 197)
16. arts and humanities (p. 196)
17. informative (p. 197)
18. Visual aids (p. 197)
19. thesis statement (p. 197)
20. discussion of main points (p. 197)

21. debate (p. 198)
22. classroom discussions (p. 197)
23. qualitative (p. 197)
24. (No answer, pp. 197–198)
25. (No answer, p. 196)
26. (No answer, p. 197)
27. (No answer, p. 197)
28. (No answer, p. 197)
29. (No answer, p. 197)
30. (No answer, p. 198)

31 *Education Courses*

TRUE/FALSE QUESTIONS

1. The most common and practical speaking event for education courses is classroom teaching.

2. A lecture is an informational speech for an audience of new student learners.

3. The classroom discussion presentation is intended as a short introduction to a group activity that follows a primary lecture.

4. Effective presentations in education require careful attention to the selection of a speech organizational pattern.

5. Successful oral presentations in education make use of examples and evidence with which the audience is familiar and can grasp.

6. Assignments in education courses often focus on some form of persuasive speaking.

7. A mini-lecture is designed to give students an opportunity to synthesize information and usually lasts fifteen to twenty minutes.

8. Lectures should always begin with a statement of the thesis.

9. Group activity presentations provide a preview of the discussion session following the activity.

10. In a classroom discussion presentation the speaker facilitates a post-lecture group activity.

11. It is important to use preview statements and transitions when giving a lecture.

MULTIPLE-CHOICE QUESTIONS

12. Sample presentations for education courses include
    A) lectures.   C) classroom discussions.
    B) group activities.   D) all of the above.

13. An effective presentation in education should
    A) always have a logical organization.
    B) separate presentation content and overall course content.
    C) ignore audience-relevant examples, evidence, and support.
    D) always have a chronological organization.

14. Which type of presentation facilitates post-lecture group activity?
    A) lecture
    B) group activity
    C) classroom discussion
    D) all of the above

15. Which type of presentation is an informative speech for an audience of new learners?
    A) lecture
    B) group activity
    C) classroom discussion
    D) all of the above

16. Which type of presentation offers brief preliminary remarks and then guides a discussion?
    A) lecture
    B) group activity
    C) classroom discussion
    D) all of the above

FILL-IN-THE-BLANK QUESTIONS

17. Types of presentations for _____ include lectures and group activities.

18. A(n) _____ is an informational speech for an audience of new student learners.

19. The _____ presentation is intended as a short introduction to a group activity that follows a primary lecture.

20. The speaker facilitates a discussion following a lecture by offering brief preliminary remarks in a _____ presentation.

21. The most common and practical speaking event in an education course is _____ .

22. Organizational devices such as _____ are used to help listeners follow ideas in a lecture.

23. A(n) _____ is designed to give students an opportunity to synthesize information in a shorter form and usually lasts about fifteen minutes.

24. When delivering a lecture you should begin with a(n) _____ .

25. When giving a _____ presentation you should first outline the critical points to be covered.

ESSAY AND SHORT ANSWER QUESTIONS

26. Name two types of education presentations.

27. Identify two characteristics of an effective education presentation.

28. How should a lecture be organized?

29. How should a group activity presentation be organized?

30. How should a classroom activity presentation be organized?

ANSWER KEY FOR CHAPTER 31

1. True (p. 199)

2. True (p. 199)

3. False (pp. 199–200)

4. True (p. 200)

5. True (p. 200)

6. False (p. 199)

7. True (p. 199)

8. False (p. 199)

9. True (p. 199)

10. False (p. 199)

11. True (p. 200)

12. D (p. 199)

13. A (p. 200)

14. B (p. 199)

15. A (p. 199)

16. C (p. 199)

17. education (p. 199)

18. lecture (p. 199)

19. group activity (p. 199)

20. classroom discussion (p. 199)

21. teaching in the classroom/ lecture (p. 199)

22. preview statements/ transitions (p. 200)

23. mini-lecture (p. 199)

24. overview (p. 199)

25. classroom discussion (p. 199)

26. (No answer, p. 199)

27. (No answer, p. 200)

28. (No answer, p. 199)

29. (No answer, p. 199)

30. (No answer, pp. 199–200)

32 Business Courses

TRUE/FALSE QUESTIONS

1. Speaking assignments in business courses often require students to understand business theory and concepts.

2. Oral presentations in business courses include informative speeches of explanation, classroom discussions, and debates.

3. Presentations in business courses are rare.

4. The most common presentation in the business course is a lecture.

5. It is not necessary to include the use of visual aids in business presentations.

6. A case study is a detailed illustration of a real or a hypothetical business situation.

7. Business presentation assignments are a great way to build your career skills.

8. In a case study presentation you should begin by discussing the background of the case.

9. Entry-level employees with superior oral presentation skills tend to get promoted sooner than their co-workers.

10. It isn't necessary to time your rehearsals when practicing for a business presentation.

11. It isn't necessary to worry about follow-up questions as your classmates are not likely to ask you questions following your presentation.

MULTIPLE-CHOICE QUESTIONS

12. In business courses, a case study presentation
    A) would never discuss a school of philosophical thought.
    B) discusses possible solutions.
    C) might explain a piece of literature, art, or music.
    D) usually deals with political leaders.

13. Sample presentations for business courses include
    A) case study presentations.   C) sales presentations.
    B) proposals.   D) all of the above.

14. An effective presentation in business should
    A) always have a logical organization.
    B) be prepared for follow-up questions.
    C) ignore audience-relevant examples, evidence, and support.
    D) always have a chronological organization.

FILL-IN-THE-BLANK QUESTIONS

15. The _____ presentation is intended to help students understand business theory and concepts.

16. Successful business presentation assignments help build _____ skills.

17. Entry-level employees with superior oral presentation skills tend to get promoted _____ than their co-workers.

18. The use of _____ has become extremely common in the workplace when giving presentations.

19. To help students understand business _____ , instructors often require them to report orally on case studies.

20. Oral presentations are just as important as _____ in business courses.

21. When doing a group project you should rehearse as a _____ .

22. Understanding the _____ of your presentation will help you understand the purpose of the presentation.

23. Follow-up questions are just as likely to come from your _____ as they are from your instructor.

24. When timing their presentations, many business students find that their presentations are much _____ than they thought they would be.

ESSAY AND SHORT ANSWER QUESTIONS

25. Explain how to do a case study presentation.

26. Identify two characteristics of an effective business presentation.

27. What kinds of presentation aids can you integrate into your business presentation? Why?

28. Why is it important to do well on your business presentation assignments?

29. Identify three types of business and professional presentations one could give in a business course.

30. Identify two characteristics of an effective group business presentation.

ANSWER KEY FOR CHAPTER 32

1. True (p. 201)	11. False (p. 202)	21. team (p. 202)
2. False (p. 201)	12. B (p. 201)	22. requirements (p. 202)
3. False (p. 201)	13. D (p. 201)	23. student-peers (p. 202)
4. False (p. 201)	14. B (p. 202)	24. shorter (p. 202)
5. False (p. 201)	15. case study (p. 201)	25. (No answer, p. 201)
6. True (p. 201)	16. career (p. 202)	26. (No answer, p. 202)
7. True (p. 202)	17. sooner (p. 202)	27. (No answer, p. 201)
8. True (p. 201)	18. presentation aids (p. 201)	28. (No answer, p. 202)
9. True (p. 202)	19. theory/concepts (p. 201)	29. (No answer, p. 201)
10. False (p. 202)	20. written assignments (p. 202)	30. (No answer, p. 202)

33 *Communicating in Groups*

TRUE/FALSE QUESTIONS

1. Group members' roles that are directly related to the accomplishment of the group's objectives and mission are called *interpersonal roles.*

2. There is no such thing as productive conflict.

3. Groupthink is the tendency of group participants to accept information and ideas only after critical evaluation and analysis.

4. Personal-based conflict is a form of unproductive conflict.

5. Issues-based conflict enhances effective decision making.

6. Counterproductive roles include "the blocker" and "the floor hogger."

7. Most negative experiences in groups result from the lack of a clear goal.

8. When member participation is unbalanced in groups, problems often arise and cause participants to be dissatisfied.

9. Effective group decision making is generally best accomplished through John Dewey's six-step process.

10. When establishing guidelines and criteria, group participants should use an interactive process that results in a consensus.

11. As group members generate solutions, the merit of each idea should be evaluated and debated immediately.

12. John Dewey contended that his decision-making process encourages group members to "think reflectively" about their task.

MULTIPLE-CHOICE QUESTIONS

13. In a group setting, "the harmonizer" and "the gatekeeper" are examples of
    A) interpersonal roles.   C) task roles.
    B) dyadic roles.   D) counterproductive roles.

14. In a group setting, "hogging the floor" and "blocking" are examples of
    A) interpersonal roles.
    B) dyadic roles.
    C) task roles.
    D) counterproductive roles.

15. Productive conflict is
    A) issues-based.
    B) personal-based.
    C) groupthink-based.
    D) motivation-based.

16. Groups prone to groupthink typically exhibit which of the following behaviors?
    A) Participants reach a consensus unwillingly, often because they don't genuinely agree with each other.
    B) Members who do not agree with the majority of the group are not pressured to conform.
    C) Disagreement, difficult questions, and counterproposals are encouraged.
    D) More group effort is spent testing the decision than rationalizing or justifying it.

17. Directly asking members to contribute, redirecting the discussion, and setting a positive tone are three techniques that group leaders can use to encourage
    A) participation.
    B) groupthink.
    C) friendship.
    D) status differences.

18. The first three steps in Dewey's group decision-making process are
    A) identify the problem, establish guidelines and criteria, generate solutions.
    B) identify the problem, generate solutions, conduct research and analysis.
    C) identify the problem, generate solutions, select the best solution.
    D) identify the problem, conduct research and analysis, establish guidelines and criteria.

19. The final three steps in Dewey's group decision-making process are
    A) evaluate solutions, conduct research and analysis, select the best solution.
    B) establish guidelines and criteria, evaluate solutions, conduct research and analysis.
    C) generate solutions, select the best solution, evaluate solution.
    D) generate solutions, evaluate solutions, select the best solution.

FILL-IN-THE-BLANK QUESTIONS

20. Group members' relational roles that facilitate group interaction are called _____ roles.

21. Group members' roles that are directly related to the accomplishment of the group's objectives and mission are called _____ roles.

22. A type of conflict in which questions are clarified, ideas are challenged, counterexamples are presented, worst-case scenarios are considered, and proposals are reformulated is called _____ conflict.

23. _____ conflict is a destructive form of conflict in which members argue about one another instead of with one another.

24. _____ is the tendency of group participants to accept information and ideas without critical evaluation and analysis.

25. _____ conflict is a type of productive conflict that allows members to test and debate ideas and potential solutions.

26. Negative or _____ roles include the "blocker" and the "recognition seeker."

27. As group members generate _____ , the merit of each idea should not be evaluated and debated.

28. In group presentations, task assignments are often linked to each member's task _____ in the group.

ESSAY AND SHORT ANSWER QUESTIONS

29. Describe three methods that you could use as a group member to discourage groupthink.

30. Explain the difference between personal-based conflict and issues-based conflict.

31. Why are both interpersonal roles and task roles important in effective group decision making?

32. Explain the steps in Dewey's decision-making process.

ANSWER KEY FOR CHAPTER 33

1. False (p. 203)
2. False (p. 204)
3. False (p. 204)
4. True (p. 204)
5. True (p. 204)
6. True (p. 203)
7. True (p. 203)
8. True (p. 203)
9. True (p. 206)
10. True (p. 206)
11. False (p. 206)

12. True (p. 206)
13. A (p. 203)
14. D (p. 203)
15. A (p. 204)
16. A (p. 204)
17. A (p. 205)
18. D (p. 206)
19. C (p. 206)
20. interpersonal (p. 203)
21. task (p. 203)
22. productive (p. 204)

23. Personal-based (p. 204)
24. Groupthink (p. 204)
25. Issues-based (p. 204)
26. counterproductive (p. 203)
27. solutions (p. 206)
28. role (p. 203)
29. (No answer, p. 204)
30. (No answer, p. 204)
31. (No answer, p. 203)
32. (No answer, p. 206)

34 *Business and Professional Presentations*

TRUE/FALSE QUESTIONS

1. Presentational speaking is generally less formal than public speaking.

2. Topics for business presentations are ordinarily chosen by the speaker.

3. In business and professional presentations, verbal interaction between speaker and audience is generally the rule rather than the exception.

4. A proposal is a presentation that gives detailed information about a procedure or device.

5. Monroe's motivated sequence offers an excellent way to organize sales presentations.

6. A staff report updates clients on developments in an ongoing market.

7. A sales presentation attempts to lead a potential buyer to purchase a service or a product described by the presenter.

8. A staff report is the same as a sales presentation.

9. A progress report is similar to a staff report.

10. The purpose of a crisis-response presentation is to reassure an organization's various audiences, not to restore credibility.

MULTIPLE-CHOICE QUESTIONS

11. Presentational speaking takes which of the following forms?
    A) reports delivered by individuals or groups in a professional or business environment
    B) individual speakers addressing a group of colleagues, managers, clients, or customers
    C) multiple members of a work group addressing a similarly composed audience
    D) all of the above

12. Sales presentations, proposals, progress reports, staff reports, and crisis-response presentations are examples of
    A) public speaking.
    C) conversational speaking.
    B) presentational speaking.
    D) ethical speaking.

13. Will gave a presentation to convince stockholders to purchase the new software he had developed. What type of presentation did Will give?
    A) a technical report
    C) a sales presentation
    B) a staff report
    D) a progress report

14. Professor Buchanan informed her colleagues about the various intercom systems she had investigated. She then recommended that the university purchase a particular system. What type of presentation did Professor Buchanan give?
    A) a proposal
    C) a sales presentation
    B) a staff report
    D) a progress report

FILL-IN-THE-BLANK QUESTIONS

15. Reports delivered by individuals or groups within the business or professional environment take the form of _____ speaking.

16. _____ speaking is generally less formal than public speaking.

17. A(n) _____ presentation attempts to lead a potential buyer to purchase a service or product described by the presenter.

18. A(n) _____ is a presentation that gives detailed information about a procedure or device.

19. Alan Monroe's _____ offers an excellent way to organize sales presentations.

20. A(n) _____ report informs managers and employees of new work-related developments.

21. A(n) _____ report updates clients or principals on developments in an ongoing project.

ESSAY AND SHORT ANSWER QUESTIONS

22. Why is there generally more verbal interaction between speaker and audience in a professional presentation than in a public speaking presentation?

23. Why is Monroe's motivated sequence effective for organizing sales presentations?

24. Describe the difference between a proposal and a staff report.

25. Discuss the elements of a crisis-response presentation.

ANSWER KEY FOR CHAPTER 34

1. True (p. 207)
2. False (p. 207)
3. True (p. 207)
4. True (p. 209)
5. True (p. 208)
6. False (p. 210)
7. True (p. 208)
8. False (p. 210)
9. True (p. 210)

10. False (p. 211)
11. D (p. 207)
12. B (pp. 208–212)
13. C (p. 208)
14. A (p. 209)
15. presentational (p. 207)
16. Presentational (p. 207)
17. sales (p. 208)
18. proposal (p. 209)

19. motivated sequence (p. 208)
20. staff (p. 210)
21. progress (p. 210)
22. (No answer, p. 207)
23. (No answer, p. 208)
24. (No answer, pp. 209–210)
25. (No answer, p. 211)